WHAT'S STOPPING YOU?

Also by Nathan D. Thomas
Be Confident in Your Creation

WHAT'S STOPPING YOU?

NATHAN D. THOMAS

journeyforth®

Greenville, South Carolina

Library of Congress Cataloging-in Publication Data
Thomas, Nathan, 1982–
   What's stopping you? / Nathan D. Thomas.
       p. cm.
   ISBN 978–1–60682–076–6 (perfect bound pbk. : alk. paper)
   1. Teenagers—Religious life. 2. Teenagers—Conduct of life.
3. Bible. O.T. Proverbs—Criticism, interpretation, etc. I. Title.
   BV4531.3.T46 2010
   248.8'3—dc22
                                  2009052191

What's Stopping You?

Design and page layout by Peter Crane

ISBN 978-1-60682-076-6

15   14   13   12   11   10   9   8   7   6   5   4   3   2   1

This book is dedicated to the past, present,
and future members and helpers
of the Leon Valley Baptist Church
Youth and Children's Ministries

CONTENTS

WISDOM'S CRY

James slammed the door to his room and threw himself on his bed. He had just finished his first week at his new high school, and already James found himself bombarded with the same temptations and obstacles he had hoped to leave behind when his family moved. Frustrated, James hit his pillow and yelled in his mind, *God, where are you? What am I supposed to do? I know what is right, but I can't do it! If you are there, why are you not helping me? Please help me!*

Life is full of obstacles that can hinder our journey for the glory of the Lord. Every day you face different obstacles in which you must choose between either living a life that pleases God or living a life that pleases yourself. Often times our failure to succeed in the obstacles of life causes us to echo the same questions that James voiced in the opening illustration. Don't be discouraged. God is present, and He desires to answer all your questions and lead you to find His will for your life in every obstacle you face. The purpose of this book is to help you find the power to overcome these obstacles and live a life that is pleasing to the Lord. The power to succeed comes only from the wisdom of God found in the Scriptures.

All Scripture is inspired by God and is filled with the wisdom of God. For our study we will focus mainly on one book of the Scriptures—Proverbs. Proverbs is perhaps the most applicable guide for the obstacles you face every day. As you take the time to read the book of Proverbs, you will understand that a main theme throughout this wonderful book is God granting the wisdom to deal with the obstacles of life. Throughout the book we will look at the top seven obstacles you will face in life and what the wisdom of God teaches about each obstacle through the inspired writings of Solomon. Before we begin our study on the obstacles of life, we need to take time to understand *wisdom's cry*. Wisdom's cry is the inspired recording of the Spirit of God's admonition and warning concerning our personal pursuit of wisdom. The Spirit of God records for us the great benefit of accepting the wisdom of God in our lives as well as the great consequences for rejecting that same wisdom. Your success or failure in overcoming the obstacles of life begins with the way you respond to wisdom's cry.

The passages referred to as wisdom's cry are found in Proverbs 1:20–33 and 8:1–21. In both passages wisdom is recorded wandering through the streets calling out to all to listen and understand wisdom. Proverbs 8 describes wisdom promising to speak of right things, excellent things, truth, and righteousness. Wisdom claims that gaining understanding is more valuable than silver, gold, rubies, and is greater than anything one can compare her to. Wisdom promises to love them that love her and to be found of them who seek for her. Upon attaining wisdom, she once again promises to grant riches and honor and to lead in the way of righteousness.

With an invitation like that, why is it that so many of us have never heard about this wisdom, and why is it so absent in the lives of Christians today? The answer to that question is found in the wisdom's cry passage in Proverbs 1:20–33. In this passage wisdom targets her cry to three categories of people: the simple, the scorners, and the fools.

In modern terms, a *simple* person is a person who loves simplicity and is easily distracted by vain pursuits. These people value the earthly riches and pleasure as greater treasure than the wealth of eternity in heaven.

A *scorner* is a person who mocks at the Scriptures and scoffs at those who would do what is right.

The definition of a *fool* has not changed and never will. This is a person who does not regard any authority or law. A fool desires only to please himself and cares nothing for others. A fool is the lowest form of life in God's eyes.

As you read the definitions of these people groups, did you notice some of the character traits exist in you? If so, then you can understand the reason why wisdom must cry for us to seek her. Honesty is difficult. Our world will tell you that you are okay, and that whatever you want to do is fine. God tells us that we are simple, scorners, and foolish. If we desire to gain the wisdom of

God for leading and directing through the obstacles of this life, our journey begins with brutal honesty.

The first step in gaining wisdom is admitting that without wisdom you are nothing more than a simple, foolish scorner. This truth is exactly why you need God's wisdom, and it is exactly why so many in our world today reject wisdom. What will you choose? Will you humble yourself or will you refuse to be honest? Before you make your choice, consider well what wisdom teaches about the two choices.

THOSE WHO REJECT WISDOM

In Proverbs 1:24–32 Solomon details the consequences of those who refuse to seek God's wisdom and rather choose to rely on their own independence. Solomon writes, "Because I have called, and ye refused; I have stretched out my hand, and no man regarded; But ye have set at nought all my counsel, and would none of my reproof: I also will laugh at your calamity; I will mock when your fear cometh . . . Then shall they call upon me, but I will not answer; they shall seek me early, but they shall not find me: For that they hated knowledge, and did not choose the fear of the Lord . . . Therefore shall they eat of the fruit of their own way, and be filled with their own devices. For the turning away of the simple shall slay them, and the prosperity of fools shall destroy them."

Heed God's Word. If you fail to humble yourself and seek wisdom, you *will* find destruction. The Spirit of God inspired Solomon to write that if you reject wisdom you will find calamity and destruction. When this takes place and you cry out for help and instruction, the Scriptures teach that wisdom will laugh at you. Ironically, you will be destroyed and killed by the very things you forsook wisdom to attain. I don't know about you, but that does not sound like a future I want to be a part of.

THOSE WHO ACCEPT WISDOM

In stark contrast to those who reject wisdom's call, those who accept wisdom's call will receive great rewards. In Proverbs 1:33, after recording the severe warning of God concerning those who reject wisdom's call, Solomon pens, "But whoso hearkeneth unto me shall dwell safely, and shall be quiet from fear of evil." Add to this promise of safety and serenity the wonderful promises of Proverbs 8, and suddenly the pursuit of wisdom becomes one of the greatest promises in God's Word. The great benefits of wisdom will be covered a little later in this book; but for now, understand the great contrast between those who reject and those who accept the call of wisdom.

The choice ought to be obvious in your mind. You can reject the call of wisdom and seek the pleasures and wealth of this world without regard for the will of God and be destroyed; or you can accept the call of wisdom and find peace, serenity, riches, honor, life, and happiness. Understand that the choice to accept wisdom comes with great rewards, but it also comes with great challenges. Your world is filled with obstacles placed by our enemy Satan to destroy your journey through this life. It is only in the wisdom of God's Word that we can find the direction to overcome these obstacles and to live a life that is pleasing to God. To gain this wisdom for victory will require much discipline in God's Word, prayer, thoughts, and outward actions.

The purpose of this book is to help you recognize and deal with some of the most important obstacles facing you in life. This book includes wisdom from God's Word for each obstacle—from the book of Proverbs in particular—that can and will help you gain the victory over each obstacle. As you read this book, I encourage you to make reading through the book of Proverbs a monthly routine in your life. You will be amazed at how many issues you face daily are dealt with in this wonderful book.

Accept wisdom's invitation, and let's begin our journey on the road to overcoming life's greatest obstacles for the glory of the Lord!

OBSTACLE 1:
INTENTIONAL IGNORANCE

WISDOM'S CRY CONCERNING WISDOM

I don't know about you, but I have a tendency to learn things the hard way. For instance:

- It was not until I had a gash in my forehead that I learned rock tag is not a fun game.

- It was not until I was cleaning up the broken glass in my parents' bedroom that I realized that using the house for second base in baseball is not a good idea.

- It was not until I was on the receiving end of a speeding ticket that I realized ignorance is not innocence.

In high school I drove a 1969 Chevrolet Camaro. I loved my car! It had a 350 high-performance vortex engine, a Richmond five-speed racing transmission, and for the exhaust I chose obnoxiously loud glass packs. I had a lot of fun with my "green goblin," as I named her, but I also got in a lot of trouble. The goblin drew the attention of any police officer within a thousand miles. On more than one occasion, I received a ticket for speeding. And I will admit that, for the most part, I deserved the tickets. However, there is one

1

particular time that I learned a very valuable lesson—*ignorance* is not *innocence*.

I was driving to the gym one night, and I decided to go a different route than usual. By this time in life, I was a Christian and truly wanted to do what was right. As I pulled onto a street, I realized I did not know what the speed limit was because I had not paid attention to the signs. So I chose to drive about forty-five miles per hour and thought that I was okay. A few minutes later I saw the lights in the mirror, so I pulled over. As the policeman approached the vehicle, I thought for sure that he would understand and realize I was innocent because I *was* truly ignorant of the speed limit. What I discovered was the opposite. Ignorance is not innocence in the eyes of justice. I received the ticket for driving 45 m.p.h. in a 35 m.p.h. zone. Though I was ignorant, I was guilty of breaking the law.

The fact that ignorance does not equal innocence is true not only in the secular world but also in the spiritual. Our world is not governed by human laws alone, but in a greater degree by the laws of God. You see, God, who created everything and rules everything, gives us specific rules and laws to obey. God placed these laws and rules in the Scriptures for us to read, learn, and understand.

Here is where the struggle begins. The world we live in is striving to cut all ties with the Scriptures. The secular world has attempted for years to discredit the Word of God (without success) and to mock all those who would place their trust in the Word. Even in the Christian realm there is a growing movement of Scriptural ignorance. Our churches have substituted psychology for doctrine, and Christians have substituted inspirational literature for the Bible. The problem is that though psychology and inspirational literature are not bad things, without the Scriptures they only contribute to the growing ignorance concerning the laws and wisdom of God.

Perhaps the greatest battlefield for wisdom today is among the youth of our churches. Teenagers are the target audience of just about everything one can imagine from music to clothing and everything in between. Sadly, the church has followed suit. Out of fear of losing teenagers to the world, the church has abandoned much of the solid teaching concerning the laws and wisdom of God and has substituted watered-down, yet flashy "outreaches" to attract teenagers.

As a youth pastor I have nothing against good outreaches and positive action to reach teenagers; but what I have noticed is what I call the "peacock movement," which means a flashy, attractive outreach that is full of activity but empty of the Scriptures. These outreaches are leaving in their wake confused and disillusioned teenagers who are losing their faith in the power and truth of God's Word.

You understand what I am talking about. Can you honestly say that you have never found yourself questioning the power and truth of God's Word as a result of some trial or situation you found yourself in? The problem is not the power or truth of God's Word; it is our knowledge and understanding of God's Word that is lacking.

I have been there. I spent years questioning God and His Word before I came to a solid understanding of the truth. If you are struggling today, allow me to encourage you not to simply read this book but rather to pour yourself into it with all your heart, seeking God for the wisdom that brings victory. The wisdom of God is the driving force behind this work and is the foundation for finding victory through all the obstacles you will face in life.

The first obstacle you must overcome is the obstacle of intentional ignorance. God gives us in His Word everything that we need to know, and for us to continue to live in ignorance is nothing more than an intentional choice to not read and study the Word of God. For you to live your life in a way that pleases God, you must know and understand what the Bible teaches concerning the different obstacles and struggles you will face. God's Word contains the wisdom you need to overcome the obstacles you face and to live in a way that is pleasing to God. Victory can be yours, but only through the knowledge and understanding of God's Word. Here is the kicker: not only will you be unable to overcome the obstacles of your teenage years and live a life that is pleasing to God if you neglect wisdom, but you will also still be accountable to God for the wisdom you intentionally ignored.

The course of action ought to be clear: you can either seek the wisdom found in God's Word and be successful, or you can remain intentionally ignorant and live a life of failure. For those of you who desire the wisdom of God's Word, let us begin our exploration into the wonderful world of the wisdom of God.

THE SOURCE OF WISDOM

In country terms, "You have got to know where the well is to get the water." If you do not know where to go to get God's wisdom, then you can have all the good intentions in the world, and you can have your wisdom buckets in hand just waiting to be filled up, but you will never attain that wisdom. Fortunately for us, the Scripture tells us exactly where to go to get the wisdom we need in order to be victorious in life. In Proverbs 9:10, Solomon writes, "The fear of the Lord is the beginning of wisdom: and the knowledge of the holy is understanding." The phrase "the fear of the Lord" occurs fourteen times throughout the book of Proverbs, and five of those times it is directly linked to knowledge, understanding, and wisdom (1:7; 1:29; 2:5; 9:10; 15:33).

For God to record a truth in Scripture just once makes it important. But God records this truth five times! There is no human analogy that can describe how important this truth must be in the eyes of God. If you want to have the wisdom of the Lord and overcome the obstacles of the teen years, then you had better develop the fear of the Lord.

There you have it. The secret to the wisdom that will make you successful in this life is the fear of the Lord!

Great. So now all we have to do is figure out what *the fear of the Lord* means. In our culture, when we think of having a fear of something, we think of fear in a negative light. For instance, I have a fear of sharks. What I mean when I say this is that I am afraid to swim in the ocean because of the possibility of a shark's finding me and eating me as lunch. I do not like sharks; I don't want anything to do with sharks. I can live a happy and satisfying life without ever coming into contact with a shark. When I think of my fear of sharks, I think of a fear that makes me want to run or stay away from what I fear. Many of you share this thinking about fear. For many of us, fear is a motivation to run away.

In the context of the Scriptures, however, the fear of the Lord is not a fear to make us run away from Him, but rather a relationship that will draw us near to Him. In modern English the "fear of the Lord" could be translated, "an awe-inspiring respect for God." How can we achieve this awe-inspiring respect for God?

I am sure you have heard the phrase, "You have to earn respect." Even though this phrase often proceeds out of the mouth of a testosterone-driven person contemplating an unwise choice, the truth of the statement stands. It is one thing to have respect for something based upon opinion and a completely different thing to have respect for something based upon experience. I can remember when the father of one of my best friends in high school purchased a brand new Corvette with all the upgrades. Loving fast cars, I immediately had a respect for the car. However, my whole view and respect for the car took on an entirely new form after I was thrown back into my seat from the force of the power of the car.

Though I had initial respect for the car, my experience with the car provided the foundation for a completely new and much deeper respect for the vehicle. In a way, our pursuit of the awe-inspiring respect of God follows the same pattern. It is one thing for us to recite the wonderful aspects about the greatness of God in a monotone distant voice. However, when we break out of the mold of religious repetition and allow our minds to fully meditate on the reality of the greatness of God through our personal experiences in life, we will begin to gain a much deeper and more real and awe-inspiring respect for God. God has earned your awe-inspiring respect already; the problem is that you are too busy simply regurgitating the truths to allow them to sink into your consciousness. Take a moment and just reflect on what God has done to earn your respect.

- God created all things, including you.

- God paid the penalty for your sin by sending His Son, Jesus Christ, to die for your sins.

- Jesus Christ, God's Son and an equal member of the Trinity, rose from the dead and is serving on your behalf on the right hand of God the Father.

- God gives us His Word to help us form a relationship with Him.

- God creates and holds in His hand every plant, animal, and insect in all creation.

- God gives you every good thing in your life.

- God provided the food you ate today and the clothes you are wearing.

- God not only created you and saved you, but He also gave you the wonderful opportunity to serve Him with your life.

This list of the greatness of God's working in your life is literally only a tiny sample of everything God does for you every single day. Do you realize that God has done so much for you? If you have never allowed the truth of the greatness of God's working in your life to sink in and produce an awe-inspiring respect for God, then now is the time. Meditate upon God and allow a genuine and deep relationship with Him to develop. God is the source of wisdom. If you desire to find the wisdom of God, then you must develop the fear of the Lord—an awe-inspiring respect. Your relationship with God requires knowledge of God found through daily Bible reading, prayer, and a deliberate and daily choice to meditate upon the greatness of God.

THE BENEFITS OF WISDOM

You may be thinking, "Hold on a second. Did you say daily Bible reading and prayer? That is hard! Do you remember what it was like to read the Bible as a teenager? Some of it doesn't even make sense. And don't get me started on prayer. I feel so lost. I don't even know if I am doing it right. How am I supposed to get motivated to gain the fear of the Lord?" If your mind is racing through similar thoughts, don't hit the panic button just yet. I do understand that forming a relationship with God takes a lot of hard work. I am not going to lie to you. Reading the Bible every day and praying every day takes a lot of time and discipline. There will be days when things go well, and there will be other days when you feel like the Scriptures don't make sense and that you must be praying the wrong way. Don't lose heart. Yes, gaining and living in the fear of the Lord is difficult, but it comes with incredible motivation!

One passage God uses to motivate us to gain wisdom through the benefits of wisdom is Proverbs 3:13–18. In this passage, Solomon, through the inspiration of the Holy Spirit, speaks about the benefits of cultivating a genuine awe-inspiring respect for God to those who choose to do the hard work. In verse 13 Solomon writes, "Happy is the man that findeth wisdom, and the man that getteth understanding." Solomon continues to write that the gain of wisdom is better than silver and the profit is better than gold. Wisdom, Solomon writes in verse 15, is more precious than jewels. Solomon states that wisdom produces long life, riches, and honor, and in verse 18 wisdom is called a "tree of life to them that lay hold upon her."

Those are some incredible promises from the Holy Spirit of God; however, there is more! Once again the Spirit of God desires to show us the great reward awaiting those who choose to step out of ignorance and into the wisdom of God found in the fear of the Lord. In Proverbs 4:5–10 Solomon lists six benefits of wisdom.

- Wisdom will preserve you (v. 6).

- Wisdom will guard you (v. 6).

- Wisdom will promote you (v. 8).

- Wisdom will bring you honor (v. 8).

- Wisdom will deliver a crown of glory on your head (v. 9).

- Wisdom will grant you long life (v. 10).

These promises are not man-made; they come directly from the Spirit of God! That means not one of these promises is false. Everything God promises to those who seek and find wisdom *will* come to fruition. Is the task difficult? Yes, but the rewards are more than enough incentive for any Christian to strive to form a deep and meaningful relationship with God that will produce an awe-inspiring respect.

Think of it in terms of a summer job. A summer job can be both a blessing and a bother in your life: a blessing because it allows you to spend your time earning money, which in turn you can invest (or spend) on whatever you want, and a bother because you might be scheduled to work when you would much rather be out at the lake. Let's say that one day your boss gathered your work crew together and presented a proposition. In this proposition, the boss asked for volunteers to perform a difficult and time-consuming task for the business. Then your boss proceeded to explain that anyone willing to do the work and fulfill the time-consuming task would be rewarded by a quadruple pay raise. In a scenario like this, who wouldn't volunteer for the task?

As incredible as this scenario is, the benefits God offers to those who would choose to step out of ignorance and into a genuine relationship with Him is a billion times better! Plus, the difficulty of the tasks—Bible reading and prayer—is a difficulty that will develop into great blessings and joy the deeper you delve in your love and respect for God. The rewards God offers you in this life range from happiness (not sold in stores), to riches, honor, long life, promotion, protection, and a crown of glory. "Hold on a second, Pastor Nate, what in the world is a crown of glory?" Good question. This reward is referring to the reward every Christian receives from the Lord for obedience in this life. We do not know for sure what it looks like or anything like that, but we do know it is a fantastic reward. Part of what makes this reward so fantastic is that the person receives this crown personally from Jesus Christ! The crown of glory may be a little mysterious, but it is definitely something you do not want to miss out on!

I cannot express to you how important it is for you to keep in front of your eyes the benefits and rewards of choosing to live in the fear of the Lord.

The pursuit of wisdom is not an easy task, but we will explore what Solomon teaches as the process for each of us to grab hold of wisdom. If you allow the difficulty of the task to keep you from gaining wisdom, then you will not only miss out on the incredible rewards and benefits of wisdom, but you will also be unsuccessful navigating the obstacles of the teenage years.

Wisdom is the foundation for your success in life. Wisdom comes only from the fear of the Lord. Acquiring this wisdom will require a full commitment on your part to work through the difficulties, keeping your eyes on the prize! So are you ready to find out how to achieve the most rewarding prize on this planet?

THE PURSUIT OF WISDOM

Success does not just happen. A person does not wake up one day and choose to be successful. You do not simply get up and march into a large corporate office building downtown, storm into the president's office, and demand a job with large pay, great benefits, and a company car. If you want to know what would happen, try it yourself. And take a friend along with a camera so we can watch you being tossed out of the building. For you to gain the vocation at the top of the food chain, you must first put in the time and earn your spot among the elite.

The same is true in the pursuit of wisdom. You do not simply wake up one day and realize that you have wisdom. If you go to sleep tonight after reading this book, there will be no wisdom fairy that will come and tap your head with her wand, granting you wisdom. If you want the wisdom that comes from the fear of the Lord and produces greater benefits than our finite minds can imagine, then you had better be willing to do some work.

In the opening five verses of chapter 2, Solomon lays out in full the process needed for you to achieve the wisdom of God. There are two words I would like you to mark in your Bible before you read this passage: *if* and *then*. For example, "if" is the third word in verse one and "then" the first word of verse five. This passage on the pursuit of wisdom is an if-then statement. What that means is that the "then" aspect of the passage is contingent on the fulfillment of the "if" aspect. If the "if" is not fulfilled, then the "then" will not come about.

Now take the free grammar lesson and read the passage. In essence, Solomon compiles an equation of actions that equals wisdom. The equation reads like this:

> IF YOU WILL receive (my words) + hiding or treasuring (my words) + making your ear attentive + applying your heart to understanding + calling out for knowledge and understanding + searching for wisdom like silver and lost treasure THEN YOU WILL understand the fear of the Lord and find the knowledge of God.

This equation reminds me a little of my senior year of high school. Entering my senior year of high school, I had a choice between two classes, either of which would fulfill my requirements for graduation—trigonometry or a freshman level math class. I chose trigonometry, which was a mistake. Up to this point I had taken algebra one and two, geometry, and a few other general math classes. Trigonometry, however, did not compute in my brain. I had equations in previous classes that used some letters; however, trigonometry brought with it whole equations of letters and a long very specific formula to find the right answer. I can remember looking with dread at those equations on tests that looked more like English papers than math and knowing that I was in for a long day.

The difference between the trigonometry nightmare and Solomon's equation for wisdom is clarity. In trigonometry, I had no idea what the letters represented and therefore I had a difficult time adding, subtracting, dissecting, and everything else I had to do to come up with the right answer. In Solomon's equation, however, it is clear that what we are adding is personal actions. The Holy Spirit does not hide or camouflage what we must do to attain wisdom. The actions are clear; the difficulty comes in taking them off the pages of Scripture and applying them in our lives.

To help aid in this process, I have listed each action in this equation with a brief explanation.

- *Receive my words*: This is accepting the Bible as the Word of God and source of wisdom. Without the acceptance in our minds and hearts that the Bible is God's Word, we will never bind ourselves to the teachings of the Bible.

- *Hide or treasure up my words*: Once you have accepted the Word of God for what it is, this second step involves taking the Word of God and storing its teachings in your heart and mind like a king would store up treasure in his castle.

- *Make your ear attentive to wisdom*: Added to the first two aspects of this equation is a willingness to hear wisdom. Often the instruction of wisdom comes in the form of teaching. If we close our ears to teaching—the instruction of wisdom—then we hinder ourselves from growing in wisdom.

- *Applying your heart to understanding*: This fourth step directly coincides with the third. You must add to the willingness to hear wisdom the desire to apply what you hear. Knowledge is great, but knowledge without application is useless. For instance, you may know that electricity and swimming do not mix well; however, until you choose to get out of the pool during a lightning storm, that knowledge will do nothing to prevent you from experiencing a shock of a lifetime.

- *Call out for knowledge and understanding*: I believe this is a call to have such an inward craving for knowledge and understanding that your desire overflows your insides, producing an outward cry for knowledge and understanding. Have you ever wanted something so badly it drove you crazy? This deep longing in your heart that dominated you is the same feeling that you should have toward the attaining of knowledge and understanding.

- *Searching for wisdom as for silver and treasure*: Following the addition of every other step comes the last admonition to go out and get wisdom. A person who desires anything to the degree that Solomon teaches will seek for it with an obsession resembling an addiction. My heart pities drug addicts. When a person is addicted to drugs, nothing matters more to that person than attaining the drug. If you want to find the fear of the Lord and gain wisdom, you must make the pursuit of it the main desire in your life. Nothing else will matter to those who are addicted to the fear of the Lord.

The Scriptures teach that if you follow this equation, you will "understand the fear of the Lord, and find the knowledge of God." Once again, we find Solomon pointing our eyes to the prize of wisdom and her benefits as motivation to persevere.

We begin this book with a chapter on the obstacle of intentional ignorance because the pervading philosophy in the world and in the church is one of biblical illiteracy. Every year it seems the world and the church replace the needful, powerful, and wisdom-packed knowledge of Scripture with the next best thing. There is nothing wrong with new programs and outreaches; however, if you replace the Scriptures, you will find yourself lacking in the God-given power to overcome the obstacles of life.

You may be in that boat. If you are honest, you may admit that you have given in to the pressure to replace the Scriptures with something new and exciting. Don't fret. Though you cannot change the past, you can change your present and future. However, this is a **choice** that you must make. You can choose to seek out the wisdom of God and alter the course of your life, or you can choose to take the easy route and crash headlong into the obstacles of life. Whatever you choose, know full well that it is you who have chosen.

If you choose to ignore the call of wisdom and remain intentionally ignorant of the Scriptures, allow me to remind you of the opening illustration. I had good intentions to obey the speed limit; I just did not know what the speed limit was. Regardless, my ignorance of the law did not keep me from the consequences of breaking the law. You may choose to remain ignorant of the truths of God's Word; however, know this—even actions performed in ignorance will result in a just punishment from God. How much happier could your life be if you would simply surrender to God and seek His wisdom. The work is hard, but the benefits you would reap in this lifetime and the next are beyond comprehension!

If you choose to reset your course for success now in your teenage years through the pursuit of wisdom in the fear of the Lord, allow me to congratulate you. You have made the first step in the journey of successful Christian living. I recommend that you honestly work through the "Charting Your Course" section below. Meditate on what you have read for the rest of the evening. Then when you have fully come to grips with your relationship with God, continue on to the next section. For it is only when you have the strong foundation of the wisdom of God that you will be willing to perform the difficult tasks that are necessary to overcome the obstacles awaiting you.

CHARTING YOUR COURSE

The Source of Wisdom

1. The fear of the Lord is the beginning of what?
2. What is a modern way to translate *the fear of the Lord*?
3. Should this awe-inspiring respect for God push us away from God or draw us near to God?
4. Make a list of several reasons that show how God has already earned this respect in your life.
5. If you have not stopped and thanked the Lord for everything He has done for you, stop and thank Him now.

Key Passage to Memorize

Proverbs 9:10

The Benefits of Wisdom

1. Review the wonderful benefits Solomon lists for those who receive wisdom from Proverbs 3:13–18 and Proverbs 4:5–10.
2. How many of these benefits can you find in stores today?
3. How many people do you know who would spend any amount of money to attain these promises?
4. Why is it so important that you keep your eyes on the benefits of wisdom?

Key Passages to Memorize

Proverbs 3:13–18

Proverbs 4:5–10

The Pursuit of Wisdom

1. Does success happen without any work?

2. Does Solomon teach that you can receive wisdom without working for it?

3. In an if-then clause, what must be performed to gain the benefits?

4. In the if-then clause in Proverbs 2:1–5, what must you do in order to gain the wisdom of God?

Key Passage to Memorize

Proverbs 2:1–5

You have the opportunity to gain the wisdom of God and live a life pleasing to Him. Will you seek this wisdom, or will you continue to live in intentional ignorance?

OBSTACLE 2:
FIENDISH FRIENDS

WISDOM'S CRY CONCERNING GODLY FRIENDS

I am a fan of college football. I love the rivalries, the upsets, and the all-round competitiveness of the schools. One of my favorite things about the college football season is "tune-up" games. A tune-up game is a game in which a powerful and talented school plays and destroys an inferior school. The purpose of these games is twofold. First, by playing a team that is not likely to beat you, the coaches are able to observe the areas that need work without the mistakes costing the team a victory. Second, these games and competitions are good for morale. Obviously the players feel more confident in their ability to have a great year if they pummel their first couple of opponents by outlandish scores.

Though tune-up games are fun to watch and be a part of (if you are on the winning side), there are no tune-up obstacles in life. The first obstacle you studied—intentional ignorance—is a difficult obstacle to overcome. However, the remaining obstacles in our study are just as difficult, if not more so. I tell you this so that you will not be surprised by the level of dedication each obstacle requires.

The next obstacle in our study is the obstacle of fiendish friends. If you think the obstacle to seek wisdom is difficult, overcoming this obstacle of fiendish friends is one of the most difficult struggles of the Christian life, especially in teenage years. The obstacle of friends is the one that seems to wreck the voyages of more Christian teenagers than any other. Victory over this obstacle is possible, but it requires a lot of work, dedication, and the wisdom of God.

Before we begin, I would like to make a deal with you. I promise that I will be completely honest with you about what the Scriptures teach concerning your friends. In return, I ask only that you are equally honest with yourself. In this chapter we will look at what the Bible teaches are good friends so that you can honestly evaluate your friends in light of the Word of God. To be successful, you must change as the Spirit moves in your life concerning specific friends. It would be a waste of your time to read this chapter and not allow the Spirit of God to work through you because of a lack of personal honesty. Do we have a deal? Let's continue.

THE BATTLE OF FRIENDSHIP

A universal rule of thumb will help illustrate the importance of this battle. The rule of thumb is this: the greater value an object has, the greater protection it receives. For instance, if you go to my favorite store, Walmart, and walk to the electronics section, you will notice several glass cases with locks on them. Inside the glass cases you will find things like iPods, video games, video game stations, portable DVD players, and other more valuable items. These items are in the glass cases because they are more valuable to the owners and potential buyers. Because of their value, the store does not want to risk the possibility of the items being stolen.

The battle for friendship is much the same. I genuinely believe that one of the greatest areas of concern for our enemy Satan is the area of friendship. Our enemy knows humans; he has been around since the beginning of humanity, and I am sure he understands the great value of friends. Because of this, the enemy places a lot of emphasis on the area of friendship. I am not going to lie to you.

This obstacle may be the greatest obstacle you face not only in your teenage years, but in your entire life. Don't allow that truth to discourage you; take heart; understand that if the enemy places his sights on the area of friendship with such passion, then it is obviously an area of potentially great rewards. Do *not* look at the difficulty of this battle, but rather at the potential rewards that victory in this battle will produce in your life. If you desire those rewards, you must fight the battle. Though the battle is great, never forget that your God and His Word are greater! Keep in mind the words of the apostle Paul, "If God be for us, who can be against us?" (Romans 8:31).

THE IMPORTANCE OF FRIENDSHIP

Why is it so important that you have godly friends? Quite simply, your friends shape who you are and what you will do. You will become your friends. Stop and read that again. The people you surround yourself with will be the people you become. You will pick up their actions, their character traits, and in many cases, their future consequences. I know what you are thinking, "Hold on, Pastor Nate. Are you telling me that my friends will change me? No, no, no, you have it all wrong. You see, *I* am going to change *them*. I am not going to do what they do; I am going to be a good testimony. Didn't Jesus tell us to witness to people? Don't worry about me; I will not give in."

Do you want to know what I call the previous statement? *Famous last words.* You see, I did not come up with the statement that you will learn your friend's traits and accept their punishment; God did. Notice what Solomon writes in Proverbs 13:20, "He that walketh with wise men shall be wise: but a companion of fools shall be destroyed." Don't stop there; go over a few pages to Proverbs 22. In verses 24–25 Solomon again writes, "Make no friendship with an angry man; and with a furious man do not go: Lest you learn his ways and entangle yourself in a snare."

I hope you noticed the common thread in these two passages. Solomon did not write, "do not be friends with fools or with angry people *unless* you plan on witnessing to them and trying to change them." Not once does the Spirit of God move Solomon to record anything other than a warning against surrounding yourself with the wrong kind of friends. In fact in both passages Solomon teaches the principle of becoming our friends. In the first passage Solomon writes that if you are friends with wise people, your own wisdom will increase. In the second passage Solomon's rationale for not being a friend of an angry person is that you will learn *his* ways and fall into a trap.

The Scriptures teach clearly, and without apology, that if you choose the wrong kind of friends, they will impact you more for evil than you will impact them for good. That is a fact; case closed; no further discussion.

God does not mince words with us, because He desires complete clarity in this biblical truth. I have been honest with you; now it is time that you get honest with yourself. If you are a person who loves to claim the *famous last words* defense of having the wrong kind of friends, it is time that you acknowledge what God says is fact. Simply put: you will not change your friends; you will become your friends. We cannot proceed any further until you accept this truth of God's Word in your heart. We are going to explore the different characteristics of fiendish friends that the book of Proverbs warns us against. However, if you have not determined in your heart to follow the counsel of God one hundred percent, then you will find yourself reasoning away whatever characteristics are present in your current group of friends. And by doing that, sadly, you will fulfill the teaching of God's Word as you become your friends.

The book of Proverbs has much to say concerning the characteristics of the people we should not call our friends. Take the following list of characteristics and references and do further research on your own time. As you read, take the time to consider what characteristics God tells us to stay away from in friends.

Fools (Proverbs 13:20)
Proverbs is full of discussions concerning the fool. There is not one single characteristic that makes a person a fool, but rather many.

Please take the time to read the book of Proverbs and mark down the different aspects of a fool.

- A person void of knowledge (Proverbs 14:7)

- A person who mocks at sin (Proverbs 14:9)

- Drunkards (Proverbs 23:20)

- Gluttons (Proverbs 23:20)

- Those who do not fear God or authority (Proverbs 24:21)

- Those with perverted speech (Proverbs 2:12)

- Those who willingly choose the paths of darkness (Proverbs 2:13)

- People who rejoice in doing evil (Proverbs 2:14)

- People who delight in perversion (Proverbs 2:14)

- People who are devious in their ways (Proverbs 2:15)

- Sexually impure people (both male and female) (Proverbs 2:16)

This list is speaking about a consistent practice. Every person is a sinner and at some time in his or her life will display some of these characteristics. This list is not meant to be a one-and-done philosophy. In other words, if a person sins once, do not check his name off your friend list. However, if there is a consistent pattern of behavior falling under one of these categories, then you must accept that the person falls under the teaching of Scripture as someone you should not be friends with.

While you were reading this list, did you think of any of your friends who display these behaviors regularly? Do you know what that is? That is the leading of the Holy Spirit showing you the people with whom you should not be friends. Before you start thinking that God is not a fair God, stop and consider the content of this list. You will not find any items that are questionable or even close to the line of decency. This list is made up of obvious sins and character traits that are arrogantly rebellious toward God and His Word. God is *not* stating that you cannot be friends with someone who likes to have fun or with someone who does not dress like the kids on *Little House on the Prairie*. What God *is* stating is that you should not be friends with people who allow wicked and dangerous sins in their life on a consistent basis.

If you want to live a life pleasing to God, then you need to end your friendships with the people of whom this list reminded you. I know it is hard, but believe me, the pain you would face in the present does not compare to the pain you will face in the future if you allow yourself to become like these people. I am *not* saying that you need to march over to their house, swing your Bible in the air, and smack them on the head pronouncing eternal judgment on their sins. What I *am* saying is that one way or another, you need to start severing ties with these people. There are many ways to do this. One of my favorite ways is to talk more openly about your beliefs and love for God. Trust me. If you start showing your love for God openly, the friends who should not be your friends will start to sever ties with you.

Think of it this way, in Proverbs 27:17 Solomon writes, "Iron sharpeneth iron; so a man sharpeneth the countenance of his friend." Hopefully by now you are willing to accept the fact that your friends will shape (sharpen) who you are. You are a Christian, and you are iron. Let's say that your friends who display bad characteristics represent the tool-sharpening materials. Your purpose in life is to please the Lord by becoming as sharp and useful for Him as possible. In light of this, what kind of material do you want to use to sharpen yourself? Would you choose to use an inferior substance such as wood, hay, or stubble in an attempt to prepare your life for the Master's use? Or, if you will excuse me, would you use dung to try and sharpen your blade? (I ask this because in honesty, you have some friends whose life is overflowing with the dung of this world, and your friendship with them is doing nothing more than taking that dung and rubbing it into your life.) Of course you would not use anything other than the finest iron to prepare your life for the Master.

I hope you grasp the power of this analogy. Why would you take the inferior elements of this world and mix them with your life when the purpose of your life is to bring glory to the Master? As silly as this sounds, spiritually speaking, this is exactly what you are doing by allowing people who do not share a love for God and His Word to surround you in life. Do you want to know why friends are so important? Friends are important because you will become your friends. As iron sharpens iron, your friends will either sharpen you for the Master's use or dull you so that you are ineffective.

GOD'S INTENTION FOR FRIENDSHIP

Every year our church hosts a fall festival for the children. This past year, I decided to break out the wood tools and paint and build several carnival games to save money. As I cut, nailed, and painted, the shape and purpose of the games began to come together. One day, however, as I was outside finishing up some of the games, a few children approached the games I had finished and began to try to figure out what their function was. As I watched, I smiled, because without the instructions, equipment, and pictures of what these games were and how they were to be used, the children could not fully understand how all the pieces worked together. It was not until they came to the fall festival and saw the proper use of the games that they realized my original intention for the games and just how amazing the games were (if I do say so myself).

After the previous section, you might be thinking that God does not want you to have any friends at all. This is obviously an errant thought. God created friendship, and He desires that you have great friendships with the right people. But just like the children and the games, we do not have the proper picture of what friendship is, and therefore we cannot fully understand just how incredible godly friendships can be. In this section we are going to look at God's intention for friendship.

God created humanity with the desire to seek out friends. God designed these friendships to provide love, care, protection, and joy throughout all situations in life. There are several passages of Scripture in Proverbs that we will look at shortly. However the best definition of God's purpose for friendship is found in Ecclesiastes, a book which is also authored by Solomon. In Ecclesiastes 4: 9,10,12

Solomon writes, "Two are better than one; because they have a good reward for their labour. For if they fall, the one will lift up his fellow: but woe to him that is alone when he falleth; for he hath not another to help him up. . . . And if one prevail against him, two shall withstand him; and a threefold cord is not quickly broken."

God intends friendships to be a source of aid and companionship in a Christian's life. A godly friend is a person we can depend on to help lift us up when we fall, both physically and spiritually. This is a great responsibility that often brings with it a time of strained relationship. Notice what Solomon writes in Proverbs 27:5–6. "Open rebuke is better than secret love. Faithful are the wounds of a friend; but the kisses of an enemy are deceitful." This passage means that if you want to be a godly friend, then when you see your fellow friend stumble, you must rebuke him or her accordingly with the goal of healing. Continue this thought. If you want to know whether you have godly friends, all you have to do is ask, "When I fall spiritually, do my friends rebuke me?" The answer to that question will help you sift through your friends. Further, ask yourself the question, "When my friends fall spiritually, do I lift them up?" Your answer will determine whether or not you are being a godly friend toward others. God intended friendships to help lift one another up when we stumble in sin.

Not only does God intend friendship to be a source of encouragement and lifting up when we are down, but God also desires that our friends be a source of comfort and love during difficult times in life. There are two passages of Scripture I want to draw your attention to. In Proverbs 27:10 Solomon writes, "Thine own friend, and thy father's friend, forsake not; neither go into thy brother's house in the day of thy calamity: for better is a neighbour that is near than a brother far off." In Proverbs 17:17 Solomon writes, "A friend loveth at all times, and a brother is born for adversity." Focus your attention on four words found in those passages: "calamity" (27:10), "all times" (17:17), and "adversity" (17:17). Each of these words indicates, either directly or indirectly, times of difficulty and trouble. Yet each time one of these words is mentioned, it follows or precedes the admonition of God concerning the friend's relationship as a means of finding solace. God intended friendships to help bring comfort and solace to us in times of great trial and sorrow.

Finally, God intends friendship to be a source of lifelong love. Look at Proverbs 18:24*b*. Solomon writes, "There is a friend that sticketh closer than a brother." What Solomon is pointing out is that a good, godly friendship will supersede time, location, and genetics. This means that it is possible for you to have a godly friendship according to the teaching of Scriptures that opens up a relationship with a person that is stronger than any amount of time in life or any distance that may separate you. This friendship may even bring you closer to that person than you are to your family members.

I made a friend in college who fits that description. Throughout college with all the ups and the downs, I shared encouragement and joy with him, and he did likewise with me. In the three years following college, I saw this friend twice, and each time was just for a brief period of time; however, my friendship with him had not dwindled at all. I still feel the same amount of love, if not more, for him as I did when we went to college together. I pray for this friend, and I look forward to one day seeing him and his wife again, even if only for a short time.

A friendship like that is the perfect illustration of what God intends Christian friendships to be. This kind of friendship will bring with it a sense of joy and love unlike anything you will experience outside of the joy of marriage. However, you will never know that kind of friendship if you continue to group people around you whom the Bible teaches should not be your friends.

Nothing can help drive the truth of the Scriptures home better than personal examples showing the truth in action in the lives of real people. So allow me to introduce you to three individuals: Amnon, Rehoboam, and Nathan. The first two are people who chose the wrong friends and suffered the consequences of their choices. The last is a man who represents a godly friend.

- Amnon

  The story of Amnon is a tragedy from start to finish and can be found in 2 Samuel 13. The story begins by informing the reader that Amnon had a sexual infatuation with his half sister, Tamar. Amnon's infatuation became so great that he literally fell into depression lusting after her. Then the author records an interesting statement in verse 3, "But Amnon had a friend, whose name was Jonadab . . . a very subtil man." As the story goes, Jonadab sees his friend in depression and upon hearing the sickening reason why he was depressed, comes up with a sure-fire way Amnon can get what he wants. In fact, it was Jonadab who gave Amnon a plan that would allow Amnon to rape his half sister. Amnon listened to the counsel of his "friend" and was murdered two years later by Tamar's brother, Absalom.

- Rehoboam

  Rehoboam's story is also tragic and can be found in 1 Kings 12. Rehoboam was the son of Solomon and successor to his father's throne. During the time of coronation, the people of Israel approach their future king and give only one request. They ask Rehoboam to lighten the tax and work load on the people, and if he will do that then they will serve him as they served his father. As the story goes, Rehoboam asks for three days to think about it. During that time he enquires with the wise men who served Solomon his father. They tell him to listen to the people and lighten the load. Then Rehoboam goes and talks with his friends. His friends tell him not only to *not* listen to the people but also to proclaim that he was going to be even harder on the people than was his father. Rehoboam listened to his "friends" and it cost him nearly all of his people.

Let's take a moment and evaluate these two examples from Scripture of what we would consider ungodly friends. In both cases the friends of these men influenced them and led them to either death or near destruction. What made these friends so dangerous to have around? First, notice that in both cases the friends cared nothing for God or for the actual well being of their "friend." These people obviously were not believers in God and cared nothing for helping their friends do what was pleasing in the sight of God. Their only concern was telling their "friend" what they thought he wanted to hear. Second, notice that from the way the Scriptures describe these friends, you could return to the list from Proverbs of what not to have in friends and find at least one of the qualities in the short description Scripture gives us. Third, notice that when the consequences for their advice came about, they were nowhere to be found. Well, that is not entirely true. Look with me at 2 Samuel 13:32. Here Jonadab, Amnon's advisor, is telling David to not mourn too much because it was only Amnon who was killed and not all the sons of David. Let me ask you, is that the kind of friend you want in your life?

- Nathan

  The last character I want to leave you with is a good example of what a godly friend should be. Nathan was a prophet who lived during the years of David's reign. There are two instances in which Nathan proved to be a genuine godly friend to the King. The first instance comes after David's sin with Bathsheba and subsequent murder of Uriah. In 2 Samuel 12 God tells Nathan to go and rebuke David for his sin. Before you start brushing this action off, remember that David was the most powerful monarch of the region. David had also been living in sin for at least nine months, maybe more. David could have easily allowed his pride and sin to take over and kill Nathan for his rebuke. However, Nathan loved God and wanted to do what was best for David. Nathan rebuked the King, and as a result David's life was spared.

  The second instance comes at the end of David's life. David was on his death bed and had yet to choose a successor. As a result one of his sons, Adonijah, decided to make himself king and conspired with Joab. Joab, Adonijah, and a whole host of Israelites went to make Adonijah king and celebrate. When Nathan heard of this, he realized the folly of it, knowing that David was going to make Solomon king. Nathan began to hatch a plan that would allow

David, his friend, to make things right for his family and lineage. Once again, notice the danger for Nathan. Joab was captain of all the army of David, a proven warrior of great skill, and the undisputed leader of the armies. If Nathan's plan did not succeed, he was as good as a dead man. Yet, once again, Nathan did not show concern for himself but rather concern for his friend. Nathan's plan succeeded and David's lineage was settled.

What made Nathan such a good friend? Two things: he loved God more than himself, and he loved David. When you have a godly friend, you will find this friend's concern is more for your well-being in the eyes of God than his or her own selfish desires. That is a godly friend. And that is what God intended friendship to look like.

Time for personal application. You know there are friends in your life that you need to deal with. You know that there are areas of your own life that are keeping your from being the type of friend that is pleasing to God. What you need to do now is confront the truth, commit to do what is right, and then do it! I know this is difficult, but remember, if the enemy did not realize how important friends are, he would not make victory so difficult to achieve. I am praying for you as I write these words. I know you can do the right thing in the power of God. The question is, *will* you do the right thing? That is a choice that only you can make, and I pray you will make the right choice.

CHARTING YOUR COURSE

The Battle of Friendship

1. How do you protect things of great value?

2. Knowing this, how do you think the enemy, Satan, feels about friendships?

3. True or False: The battle over friendship is great but God is greater!

The Importance of Friendship

1. Your friends are important because _____ will become your _____.

2. Why do I refer to the statement "I can change my friends" as famous last words?

3. What analogy does Solomon use in Proverbs 27:17 to show the importance of the people you surround yourself with?

4. Look at the list of the kinds of people God does not want you to be friends with. Do you have friends that consistently display these attributes?

5. If so, what material are you using to sharpen your iron?

6. What do you need to do to stay sharp for the Lord?

7. How are you going to do this?

God's Intention for Friendship

1. In what book do we find God's written intention for friendship? (Hint: there are sixty-six books in this one book.)

2. If you do not read this book, will you know what God wants friendships to look like?

3. Why did Amnon's friend, Jonadab, make such a bad friend?

4. Where was this man Jonadab after Amnon was murdered?

5. What advice did Rehoboam's friends give him?

6. What did this advice cost Rehoboam?

7. What two characteristics made Nathan a godly friend?

8. True or False: A godly friendship stands no matter the time or distance separating the two individuals.

Personal Evaluation

1. What kind of friend am I to others?

2. What can I do to make myself a better godly friend to those who are depending on me?

3. What areas do I need to change in my own life?

4. In what ways am I already displaying the sinful characteristics of my friends?

5. Record the names of the friends that the Spirit of God is dealing with me about.

6. Do these friends you listed help sharpen you for the Master's use or dull you?

7. What am I more afraid of, displeasing my friends or displeasing God?

OBSTACLE 3:
SEXUAL
SEDUCTION

WISDOM'S CRY CONCERNING SEXUAL PURITY

Have you ever been in a situation in which something *needed* to be addressed but no one wanted to talk about it? I found myself in a situation like that one year as a Christian camp counselor. I had only a few rules in my cabin outside of the camp's mandatory rules. On this night, the one rule that obviously had been broken was the rule I had for the toilet: "If you clog it, you clean it." As I walked into the cabin, it was clear from the overflowing porcelain chair, the unique aroma, and the guilty look on everyone's face that this rule had been breached. Every boy in that cabin knew it, and I came to find out that every boy in that cabin knew who broke the rule. Yet no one wanted to address what so obviously needed addressing.

In Christian circles, the area that needs to be addressed—even if no one really wants to—is the area of sexual purity. The truth is, and it is obvious to any teenager reading this book, that our world is dominated by sexual seduction. Our world abuses sexuality to sell any and all products, to attract viewers for television ratings, and to make fortunes in the pornography industry. From magazines to the internet, from television and movies to billboards, our world is abusing sex. This is *our* world, and if we refuse to address this problem as Christians, then we are only setting ourselves up for an inevitable fall into sin.

We saw in the last chapter that the consequences for wrong friendships can be devastating, but there is no sin in life that carries such a destructive and life-changing power as that of sexual immorality. If you desire to live your life in a way that is pleasing to God, then you must acknowledge, prepare for, and overcome the obstacle of sexual seduction.

As we begin the exploration into what the Scriptures teach concerning sexual purity, I want to take a moment and warn you about this battle. So many of the battles we face in the Christian walk can be handled through spiritual and mental discipline alone. In the battle for sexual purity, however, a new enemy comes into play: our bodies. God created your body to desire and enjoy sexual relationships inside the vows of marriage. As a result, the world's abuse and promotion of sinful sexuality will appeal to your body. The more you allow this sin and these actions to stay in your life, the stronger your desire for them will become. You need to understand this because so often Christian teenagers get confused about the power of the enemy and the power of God's Word to deliver because of the seeming inability to gain the victory over their own desires and feelings. If you find yourself in this boat, allow me to encourage you that victory *is* possible, but you can achieve this victory only through the power of God in the disciplining of your mind, body, and soul.

THE TIMELESS STRUGGLE OF SEXUAL PURITY

When I was nine years old, I lost my right eye in an accident. Ever since that time I have struggled dealing with this "affliction." One reason why I struggled so much is that I did not know anyone else who could understand. I was the only person I knew with just one eye. Even after salvation and spiritual growth, talking with people who have lost an eye is still one of the best sources of encouragement. The encouragement I gain from talking with others is not always spiritual or deep but rather just encouraging to know that

I am not the only person who deals with the inner turmoil and struggles of this life.

The first aspect about the battle for sexual purity I want you to grasp is the fact that you are not the first and not the only person to struggle in this area! In fact, from the beginning of the infusion of sin into the human race, men and women have struggled and failed in this most devastating trap of the enemy. The danger of this battle is that it has no age boundaries. When you hit twenty, you will still struggle with this battle. Adults still battle with this obstacle. Think about it, if this obstacle only affected a few select individuals like yourself, then there would not be such a tremendous emphasis on sex in the markets all over the world. This obstacle of sexual temptation is not unique to you, but rather it is common among nearly all teenagers and adults all around the world. Take a moment and think of the many different biblical characters who struggled against this great obstacle.

- Job made a covenant with his eyes to not lust for other women. (Job 31:1)

- Joseph was tempted by Potiphar's wife. (Genesis 39)

- The children of Israel participated in illicit sexual activities with the children of Moab in their journeys. (Numbers 25)

- Judah looked for a prostitute and slept with his daughter-in-law. (Genesis 38)

- Lot's daughters committed incest with their father. (Genesis 19)

- Samson's greatest weakness was his unchecked sexual desires. (Judges 13–16)

- King David's greatest weakness was women. His sexual lust for Bathsheba was a low point in his life. (2 Samuel 11–12)

- King Solomon had more wives and concubines than you can imagine. When he was old, they turned his heart away from God. (1 Kings 11)

- Paul wrote a letter to the church at Corinth to deal with a man who slept with his father's wife. (1 Corinthians 5)

Did you realize the Scriptures provided so many stories about real people who shared the struggle of sexual seduction? In one of my favorite passages, the apostle Paul reminds us that we are not alone in our struggle with sin, no matter what sin it might be. In 1 Corinthians 10:13 Paul writes, "There hath no temptation taken you but such as is common to man: but God is faithful, who will not suffer you to be tempted above that ye are able; but will with the temptation also make a way to escape, that ye may be able to bear it." Notice three life-changing truths the Holy Spirit gives us from this verse.

1. You are not alone in your temptation. (Sound familiar?)

2. Though God does not tempt us, God does set boundaries for the tempter so that he does not tempt us more than we can bear.

3. In every situation God faithfully provides us with the power and opportunity to say no (to escape) and to be able to endure.

I encourage you to memorize 1 Corinthians 10:13 and the three coinciding truths. When you are in the heat of battle, this truth from God's Word has the power to help you overcome even the fiercest of obstacles. Take the advice of the Psalmist who wrote in Psalm 119:11, "Thy word have I hid in my heart, that I might not sin against thee." There is no obstacle that can stand against the power of God's Word.

You are not alone in your struggle with sexual seduction. From the beginning of sin in the human race, an innumerable host of men and women have struggled with this fierce obstacle. Allow that truth to comfort you. You are not odd, or weird, or troubled. You are a human with a flesh nature just like the rest of us. But before you get too comfortable with your struggles, remember the truths of 1 Corinthians that teach there is no excuse for falling into temptation because God always provides a way to overcome. This is the first step to gaining the strength from God's Word to overcome. The second step, and perhaps the most motivational step, comes as we discover the truth concerning the lasting effects of sexual sin.

THE ENDLESS CONSEQUENCES OF SEXUAL IMMORALITY

I grew up in rural Oklahoma. As a child I was as rough and tumble as they come. One of my favorite activities was to chase down creatures and capture them in jars, buckets, or anything else I could find. I always loved going to see my father's parents because they lived deep in the country, and we could always find cool creatures to capture. One day, however, our fun turned dangerous. There was a large tree in my grandparent's yard which lizards loved to crawl around. If you are familiar with country habitats, trees also attract predators who feed on the insects and animals that live on and around trees. In other words, the fun came with a risk. That day we chose to neglect the risk and focus only on the fun. As I chased a rather large lizard near the tree, I stepped on something that made me jump back. It was a copperhead snake, and I made it extremely mad to say the least. Soon I found myself calling for help as the snake began to chase me. Fortunately for us our parents and grandparents were keeping an eye on things and were able to come and kill the snake before it took it revenge on a silly little boy. Needless to say, the allure of the fun of the tree lost its effect on me, and I stayed inside the entire rest of the day!

Our battle with sexual seduction has a lot of similarities with this incident. You already know that sexual sins can be temporarily fun, exciting, and pleasing. If there was no temporary pleasure in sexual sins, then the obstacle would not be nearly as dangerous and overwhelming. If the experience were about the same as smashing your hand in the car door, then we would likely not have to cover this obstacle in this book. Sexual sins seem fun and desirous to our flesh. However, like my story, the temporary fun comes with a great risk.

The consequences for sexual sin are devastating and endless. Other than the impact your sin will have on your relationship with God, the consequences of your sin in this life are the greatest motivating factors to seek sexual purity. Before we go there, however, let me explain one extremely important breakdown from the analogy of the tree and snake. In my experience, I did not suffer the bite of the snake; I got away unharmed. When you commit sexual immorality, however, there is no escape from the consequences. Though you might be able to hide your actions from anyone's knowledge (and that's not likely), the inner damage has already taken place. That is the terrifying truth about sexual immorality. Solomon writes that it is not like any other sin you can commit, because it is a sin that damages your very soul (Proverbs 6:32).

The book of Proverbs speaks on the sin of sexual immorality in four major passages (2:16–19; 5:3–23; 6:24–35; 7:5–27). We are going to deal with two of these passages in this section and look at how the passage in Proverbs 7 can help us understand the pattern that leads to failure or success in dealing with this obstacle. There is some overlap in these passages concerning the consequences of sexual immorality; however, there are two major consequences of sexual immorality that Solomon records. Please read these passages in their entirety as we look at them individually.

Proverbs 5:3–23 — Endless Regret

Regret. There is no misunderstanding about the endless regret that accompanies sexual immorality. Focus on what Solomon writes regarding this regret in verses 11–13 of Proverbs 5: "And thou mourn at the last, when thy flesh and thy body are consumed, And say, How have I hated instruction, and my heart despised reproof; And have not obeyed the voice of my teachers, nor inclined mine ear to them that instructed me!"

Do these words sound like words of someone who is proud of his or her actions? Of course not, and yet the world tries to convince you that sexual immorality is fun and exciting. Your friends (who, after our study in the last chapter, should not be your friends) prod you to lose your virginity and "have some fun." Wisdom, however, warns that those who choose to participate in such actions will receive a regret that will not fade until they close their eyes in death. Notice the time of life for the individual mentioned in this passage. Verse 11 states that this statement comes at the end of the person's life. In other words, these are the words of a man or woman on his or her deathbed. There is no telling how long ago the sexual immorality took place. What we do know is that at the end of life, the regret remains.

The regret sexual immorality brings is a heavier burden than you can imagine! I watched friends in high school think they were doing the cool thing and ending up falling into deep depression with suicidal tendencies. I have watched as men studying to go into the ministry, whose gifts far exceeded anything I could ever hope to attain, lose everything because of failure to overcome this obstacle. I have also watched the devastation of sexual immorality plunder the joy from the lives of teenagers under my ministry, leaving their families and futures in disarray. If I could gather all of these people together and stand them in your presence, the one thing they would share with you is the hellish regret that fills their hearts and minds.

God can and will forgive you for sexual immorality. The Bible is clear on that subject. Though forgiveness is wonderful, the consequences of your actions will remain lodged in your heart and mind. Is forgiveness available? Yes, praise God it is, and I pray that if you have fallen into this sin you would not spend any more time living without forgiveness. But do not miss the fact that the only way for you to be free from the devastating, endless regret of sexual immorality is to remain sexually pure.

Proverbs 6:24–35 — Endless Guilt

This last consequence Solomon mentions may seem to coincide with the previous consequence. The difference comes not in feelings but in actions. Read with me Proverbs 6:27–29, 33. Solomon teaches that just as a man who carries fire in his arms will get burned, and just as a man who walks on coals will get his feet burned, so every man and woman who commits sexual immorality will be guilty. Verse 32 picks up that thought and continues to reveal that the person will receive a wound and dishonor and his or her reproach will not be wiped away.

An illustration will help you put this truth in modern context. Let's say a man is arrested for sexually abusing a child (horrible). The jury decides not to kill this man (mistake) and sentences him to several years in prison. In prison the man gets saved (miracle) and changes his life around. Upon release from prison, the man is a new person and completely different from the monster who committed the sexual act. Regardless, wherever the man goes for the rest of his life, he will have to register as a sex offender. No matter how different the forgiveness of God has made this man, the victim's family will always remember what he did. His sexual actions will leave a reproach and dishonor on his name that no amount of good deeds or personal forgiveness can change. He is, and forever on this earth will be, a sex offender.

When you choose to commit sexual immorality, you are guilty of being a sex offender. God can and will forgive you for your sin and wipe you as clean in His eyes as if you had never sinned. However, for as long as you are alive, your sexual offense will live with you. For as long as the other person(s) involved have memory, your offense will remain. You will be forever guilty of being a sex offender.

As we discussed these consequences outlined by Solomon, you might be thinking, "That does not sound fair! Why should one mistake, one sin, cause such lasting consequences? It is just not fair!" In one sense I will agree with you that it seems harsh; however, that is exactly why God gives us so much warning in His Word to abstain from sexual immorality and be sexually pure. These consequences are reality. If you take nothing else with you from this chapter, take this following principle: sexual immorality brings at best *temporary* pleasure but leaves at least *endless* consequences.

It is like Solomon's analogy. A person who plays with fire gets burned. The skin that is burned will always reveal the results of the burn in scarring and deformity. The person who plays with sexual immorality will have with them the scars revealing the incident for as long as they inhabit their bodies. Please, do not suffer the horrible and life-changing consequences of regret and guilt in order to gain a temporary thrill!

The consequences we have covered are terrible and ought to be enough motivation for you to commit sexual purity. These consequences are terrible, but note that these are not the only consequences you risk when you allow sinful sexual practices in your life. I did not even mention STDs, AIDS, and pregnancy out of marriage. These are all real risks that you take when you give in to sexual seduction.

THE PATTERN FOR FAILURE AND SUCCESS IN PURSUIT OF SEXUAL PURITY

Thus far we have looked at the battle raging over sexual purity and the consequences accompanying sexual immorality. We will conclude with a pattern that will lead to your success or failure in this battle. "That sounds odd," you might be thinking. "How can one pattern lead to both success and failure?" I am glad you asked . . . or read the question anyway. I would love to show you the pattern for success and failure as given to us by Solomon in Proverbs 7.

In Proverbs 7:6–9 Solomon records the events he witnessed one evening. Within the details of this account is the pattern for success and failure. Notice with me what Solomon sees. Solomon recounts seeing a man walking through the street *near her corner* and going in the *way toward her house*. Not only was this man walking in this place, he was also walking in the *twilight* in the *black and dark night*. Notice what the italicized words tell us. The man was in the wrong place (*near her corner*) with wrong intentions (*toward her house*) at the wrong time (*twilight, the black and dark night*). To help us cognitively grasp this let's change the order: the man was in the wrong place at the wrong time with the wrong intentions. As a result, he found exactly what he was looking for, and the Scriptures read that what he was looking for led him away like an ox to the slaughter.

The pattern for failure looks like this.

$$^{\text{wrong}}[\text{place}] + {}^{\text{wrong}}[\text{time}] + {}^{\text{wrong}}[\text{intentions}] = \text{FAILURE}$$

Now let's take this formula and change one word. Instead of being in the wrong place, put yourself in the *right* place. Instead of the wrong time, go during a *right* time; instead of having wrong intentions, commit to *right* intentions.

That means the pattern for success looks like this.

$$^{right}[\text{place}] + {}^{right}[\text{time}] + {}^{right}[\text{intentions}] = \text{SEXUAL PURITY}$$

All right, let's drive this point home. If you know there is an event where you will not have appropriate supervision over your interactions with the opposite sex, that is the wrong place. Stay away from those places and situations and you are more than halfway on the road to success! Think about it, if you keep yourself from being in the places where you will have the opportunity to fall, your chances of remaining pure skyrocket! Don't go to the wrong places, and you will have the advantage.

Second, when it comes to guarding the right time, never forget your adversary is always looking for a way to trap you. Just because you make the commitment to not go where you should not go does not mean the enemy will give up on you. Keep this in mind, because it is needful for anyone wanting to live sexually pure to be on guard all of the time. You may not be in a place that you consider the wrong place; however, any place can turn into the wrong place if the time is the wrong time. The wrong time can be anytime in which proper godly supervision is not present. That can take place day or night, on week days or weekends. The main principle to ensure about the right time is always check on supervision. Whenever there is not sufficient supervision or accountability, it is the wrong time!

Third, if you have the wrong intentions, you will find what you are looking for. And what you find will destroy your life. To prevent this, make a commitment with God that you intend to stay sexually pure. Without the right intentions, you will lead yourself to the corner near the house of sin, and you will meet with the person of sin you are looking for. However, if you choose from the beginning to remain pure for God, for your spouse, and for your family, you will have the advantage over the enemy.

The pattern of right place + right time + right intentions will lead to purity. However, be warned that even if you are lacking in only one of these areas, it can lead to failure. Follow the right pattern and prepare for the fight to overcome sexual seduction by hiding

God's Word in your heart. In the application section of this chapter there will be several passages you need to look up to record what they say about the battle you are in. Do this well; memorize these passages; arm yourself with the Sword of the Spirit to defeat your enemy.

As we conclude this chapter it is necessary to remember that as in any other struggle, the choice to be victorious rests in your hands. God gives us His Word and His power to overcome temptation, but He leaves the choice to us to take up arms and fight for purity. You can live a life that is pleasing to God and remain sexually pure; however, that comes as a result of you disciplining your body, mind, and soul in the power of God's Word. There is no other battle you will face that has such high stakes. Victory brings peace, joy, and a clear conscience. Defeat brings endless regret and guilt. Which will you choose?

Never forget, sexual immorality brings at best *temporary* pleasure but leaves at least *endless* consequences.

CHARTING YOUR COURSE

The Timeless Struggle for Sexual Purity

1. How does knowing you are not the only person to battle with sexual purity make you feel?

2. Name the listed biblical characters that succeeded in their battle with sexual purity.

3. How did their lives turn out?

4. Name the listed biblical characters who failed in their battle with sexual purity.

5. How did their lives turn out?

6. Which of these characters do you want to be like?

7. Read the following Scriptures and record what they say concerning your battle with sexual purity.

    a. 1 John 1:9

    b. Matthew 5:27–28

    c. Proverbs 6:16–18*a*

      d. Psalm 103:10–12

      e. Psalm 101:3

      f. 1 Corinthians 10:13

      g. Psalm 119:11

Key Passage to Memorize

    1 Corinthians 10:13

The Endless Consequences of Sexual Immorality

1. Solomon records two consequences that never end from sexual immorality:

    a. Endless _____

    b. Endless _____

2. Can you find forgiveness for your sin if you commit sexual immorality (1 John 1:9)?

3. Can you control the consequences of your sexual immorality?

Key Passage to Memorize

    Proverbs 6:27–29

The Pattern for Failure and Success

1. The pattern for failure places you in the _____ place at the _____ time with the _____ intentions

2. The pattern for success places you in the _____ place at the _____ time with the _____ intentions

3. Whose responsibility is it to keep you out of the wrong place at the wrong time with the wrong intention?

4. List all the places you need to stay away from.

5. What makes any time the wrong time?

Key Passage to Memorize

    Proverbs 7:6–9

OBSTACLE 4:
LIFELESS LIVING

WISDOM'S CRY CONCERNING TIME MANAGEMENT

I love laser tag! Laser tag is one of my favorite youth group activities. What I love about this game is that to win, you must play with intensity the *entire* twenty minutes. If you slack off for even a little bit, you could find yourself coming in the bottom of the rankings. In order to be successful in laser tag you have to do three things: be productive, understand your role, and always be aware of the time.

For you to live a life that is pleasing to God, you also must follow these laser tag rules: be productive, understand your role and how God views your life, and always be aware of the brevity of life. The problem is that the normal Christian's life is not nearly as intense and distraction-free as a game of laser tag.

In real life there are numerous distractions that vie for your time and energy. In the world you live in, there is an incredible array of entertaining distractions. These distractions take the form of intense and realistic video games, social interactions and networks on the internet, and a never-ending supply of movies. Add to these distractions television shows, jobs, summer activities, extracurricular activities, and good old-fashioned wasted time, and you have just summarized the whole of the average teenager's life (except for eating, which they do a lot). There are two major problems with this list: everything spiritual is left out, and nothing that will last for eternity is present.

This is the problem. The world distracts the Christian teenager through the entirety of his or her waking hours with useless and vain activities. The teenager does not see the danger, because it is not like they are denying God or anything. However, while they remain in the grasp of vanity, they waste their teenage years and accomplish nothing for God. This fact has devastating consequences on Christianity and individuals.

The church is a living organization that requires dedicated and active members to fulfill its biblical mandate. When the youth of the church become distracted with all the other pursuits of this world, often the first thing to go is their participation in the church activities.

This fact not only causes harm to the church, but in a greater way it is destroying the lives of the teenagers involved. You as a Christian need to be plugged in to the Word of God, prayer, and your local youth ministry. These venues in many cases are your only lifeline for spiritual nourishment. The more time you spend away from them, the more spiritually malnourished you become. This process over time will weaken you to the point that your guard against sin and your sensitivity and desire for God are gone. I have witnessed more than a few teenagers get so entangled with the distractions of this world that they lose their zeal, purpose, and perspective, and they spend their lives living lifeless existences.

Lifeless living is a universal problem. I would be shocked if you could honestly say that you do not see the distractions of this world beginning to choke the spiritual life out of some area of your walk with Christ. Solomon is honest with us; I will be honest with you; but for the Word of God to make a difference in your life, you must be honest with yourself. Once again, success in this obstacle requires your honesty.

LIFELESS LIVING IS BARREN LIVING

Throughout this discussion, as well as throughout the Scriptures, we will continue to come across a term that you might not be familiar with. The term is *sloth*. The word sloth is synonymous with laziness, idleness, sluggishness, inactivity, and apathy. It is also the term the Holy Spirit uses to define people who live a lifeless life. It is not a term that anyone in his right mind would want to be used to define him as a person. Yet, sadly, sloth is the way that many Christian teenagers appear in the eyes of God.

Turn your attention to nature for better understanding. There is an animal called a sloth. The three-toed sloth is a fascinating animal to watch. It is not fascinating for any reason that would make you want to pretend to be one, but it is fascinating because it is almost painful to watch them move. Part of the way sloths defend themselves is to blend in with trees. This camouflage is effective because they move at such a slow rate of speed that normally the leaves will move more in the wind than the sloth does! These creatures do little more than eat, sleep, and once a year mate. That is it! That is the entire being of a three-toed sloth. We don't know for sure if the Spirit of God wanted to relate the slothful person to a three-toed sloth, but what we do know is that the slothful person is condemned in the Scriptures for having characteristics that relate to the unattractive animal. Being called a sloth is not a compliment, and yet it is the title that God gives to those who live life caught up in the distractions of this world to the neglect of God's work.

The first step you must take in order to overcome the obstacle of lifeless living is to make your life productive. In order to help you gauge your productivity for the Lord, we are going to look at the characteristics of the sloth. Be aware that these characteristics are counterproductive. If you recognize any of these characteristics, then understand in honesty that you are likely living a lifeless life.

Characteristic Number 1: Laziness

The first characteristic of slothfulness is laziness. It is interesting how the progression of teenager responsibilities have evolved throughout this past century. It used to be that when a boy hit his teenage years, he would be responsible to help his father with the burdens of the family. Often this was seen in his doing chores around the family farm or garden or hiring out for labor in a warehouse in the city. This work ethic was the normal routine for anyone outside the upper tier of society. Today, however, things are different! Teenagers are allowed to be lazy, useless, and completely noncontributing to their families or society. This lack of expectations upon teenagers today has allowed an attitude of laziness to flourish as the norm.

Though the world's expectation for the American teenager is increasingly lax, God's expectations for you have not changed. God's Spirit inspires Solomon to rebuke the attitude and practice of laziness throughout the book of Proverbs. Keep in mind, though the world might not expect much of you, God's expectations reign supreme.

The passage I want you to read is Proverbs 21:25–26a. In this passage from the Spirit of God, Solomon writes, "The desire of the slothful killeth him; for his hands refuse to labor. He coveteth greedily all the day long." The picture given in these verses is pathetic, and yet it is an accurate portrayal of slothfulness. Solomon describes a person whose love and desire for nice things literally drives him crazy. This person craves and craves these things, but will never attain them. The reason this person craves without ever achieving is because the person refuses to work. Note, the passage did not say *could not* work, but rather refuses to work. That is called laziness.

Laziness can and will destroy your physical and spiritual life. Further, laziness is a growing epidemic in the ranks of the church. All throughout this wonderful book of Proverbs, Solomon records aspects of laziness such as a love of sleep, constant idleness, a refusal to work, and a choice to follow after "vain persons." Now take these descriptions and compare them to the attitudes, events, and daily routine of your own life. There are probably more similarities in this comparison than there ought to be. Perhaps you have never considered the time you spend on entertainment or recreation to be an outward display of laziness. Perhaps you never considered the large amount of time you spend on video games, movies, and social networking to be harmful at all. I do not think all time used in the previous actions is an indication of laziness; I am speaking to the spending of large quantities of time.

The question you need to ask is how much time do these activities take away from beneficial work? I am not only writing about physical work, but more importantly spiritual work. Compared to the time you spend on video games, movies, and social networking, how does your time in God's Word measure up? What about the time you spend in prayer? What about the time you spend witnessing, going to youth functions, and fulfilling God's commission on your life? Here comes the honesty question. Is the comparison embarrassing? How do you think God sees your life for Him? Do you think God sees you as a faithful and diligent worker or a lazy sloth more concerned about empty and vain things than working the work of eternity? Don't allow laziness to rule your life!

Characteristic Number 2: Full of Excuses

The second characteristic of a spiritual sloth is that he always has an excuse. Teenagers who struggle with slothfulness always seem to have some sort of excuse to explain their sinful actions. There is always someone, something, or some event that bears the true blame in their stead. I must be old-fashioned, but one thing I was always taught—whether it was by my father or an athletic coach—was never make excuses! I read a humorous article the other day in which the author explained that if he ever had to go to court, he would not hire an attorney, but rather would have his teenage son defend him. His reasoning was that his son seemingly has an endless supply of excuses and reasons why he is unable to do what his father requires of him. The point of the article is to demonstrate that the world accepts and, in a greater way, expects excuses from teenagers. The article was light-hearted, but the truth that the article exposes is anything but funny in God's eyes.

The use of excuses is a major theme in the writings of Solomon concerning the sloth. Read a list of the excuses Solomon records through the Spirit of God that fill the mind and mouth of the sloth.

- Can't work because of the weather (Proverbs 20:4)

- An unfounded fear (Proverbs 22:13, 26:16)

- Hanging out with friends (Proverbs 12:11)

- His own "wisdom" (Proverbs 26:16)

Two of the listed excuses are humorous. The slothful man in Solomon's writings states that he cannot go out and be productive because there are lions out in the world. Is that true? Yes. There are lions. Is that a valid excuse not to work? Absolutely not. Just as this excuse is ridiculous, so are many of the excuses we make in order not to serve God. We say, "There are mean people in this world who don't want to hear about Jesus; therefore I can't go and tell people about Jesus." Is it true that there are some people in this world who do not want to hear? Yes, but should we allow the few people who might cause problems keep us from doing our work? Absolutely not. Yet we hide behind the excuses of this life, whether the excuses are work, games, friends, or our own wisdom, and we refuse to do the labor God gives each of us to do.

The last passage listed, Proverbs 26:16, is a revealing verse. Solomon writes, "The sluggard is wiser in his own conceit than seven men that can render a reason." This verse makes me picture many Christian teenagers who make excuses based on their own wisdom; wisdom that is contrary to God's Word and the teaching of God's men. If you hold on to excuses to explain your own slothfulness, then know that you are living in contradiction to the desire of God. Your excuses, as grand as they may seem to you, are nothing more than foolishness in the eyes of God. The only thing your excuses accomplish is keeping your life barren in the eyes of God.

Characteristic Number 3: A Barren Harvest
The last characteristic we will look at in the life of the sloth is the most devastating truth concerning the lifestyle. The end result of such a life is a barren harvest. This means that all the activities that the person poured his or her entire life into produced nothing for the Lord. This end result, standing before the Lord and watching

your entire life work go up in flames, is a tragedy that no Christian ought to experience. This ending is in fact the entire foundation behind the warning of Scripture—as well as the warning of this book—that you not find yourself barren in the day of judgment.

Though there is no phrase or warning that could do justice to the great devastation a barren harvest would bring, Solomon gives us a wonderful picture from nature to help us understand what the life of the slothful produces in Proverbs 24:30–34. "I went by the field of the slothful, and by the vineyard of the man void of understanding; And, lo, it was all grown over with thorns, and nettles had covered the face thereof, and the stone wall thereof was broken down. Then I saw, and considered it well: I looked upon it, and received instruction. Yet a little sleep, a little slumber, a little folding of the hands to sleep: So shall thy poverty come as one that travelleth; and thy want as an armed man."

In this wonderful account of the observations of Solomon is the honest truth concerning the productivity of the slothful in the eyes of God. Solomon describes a vineyard owned by a sloth. This vineyard was not producing grapes as is its purpose, but is instead producing nothing. The reason is that the vines are not dressed or cared for, the ground is not cleaned or weeded, and the stone wall set up to protect the fruit of the harvest is broken down, allowing anything and everything to destroy the vineyard.

This is a sad picture. What makes this picture sad is the fact that the vineyard is a reflection of many Christian teenagers' spiritual lives. This might even be a reflection of your spiritual life. Christian teenagers fill their lives with activities that produce nothing for the Lord. Because of their obsession with games, movies, social networking, and their neglect of their spiritual responsibilities, their lives resemble this vineyard—undercared for, overgrown, unprotected, and most devastatingly, barren!

What kind of life are you living for God? Are you producing fruit for the Savior, or are you wasting your time following the vain pursuits and pleasures of this world? Understand that you cannot do both and accomplish what God desires for your life. Yes, it is okay to spend some of your time in recreation and entertainment;

however, when your pursuits of recreation and entertainment hinder your production for the Lord, you are neglecting your spiritual vineyard. To neglect your spiritual vineyard will lead to a barren harvest for the Lord. And that is an end that will stay with you for all eternity.

So far we have looked at the three characteristics of the lifeless, barren life. As we continue, we are now going to examine what the Scriptures teach is God's view of the sloth.

GOD'S VIEW OF THE SLOTH

The formula for success begins with productivity. As we just examined, the characteristics of the sloth make it impossible to be productive. The second step in the formula to be successful is to understand your role and responsibilities. For this we look not at what the world thinks of the sloth, but what God thinks of the sloth. Of the two, God's view is the view that reigns supreme, and therefore it is the view we must concern ourselves with.

In Proverbs 18:9 Solomon writes, "He also that is slothful in his work is brother to him that is a great waster."

Read that verse again. God places the slothful person in the same family as a great waster. God is stating that a person who lives his or her life displaying the characteristics of a sloth is equal to a person who goes through life wasting opportunities and blessings. When I think of a great waster, I think of an ungrateful person who is a poor steward of what he has, but he does not care. Why would God compare the two types of people and group them together?

The answer can be found in the responsibilities of the Christian. I will not record the passage for you, but the perfect explanation of God's feeling toward the sluggard is found in the parable of the talents in Matthew 25:14–30. In this wonderful parable from the lips of God comes the understanding that God gives each of us gifts and talents that He desires we put to use for Him. When we do that and work for our Lord, we will receive a reward in heaven. However, if we choose to take the slothful route and bury our talents in the sand of laziness and vain pursuits, then we will one day receive a great rebuke for wasting our opportunities. Understand that God gives you every blessing and gift you have for a purpose. For you to refuse to use it for Him and gain treasure for the Lord is a waste! There is no middle ground. God either sees you as a faithful worker or a great waster. Notice that the servant in the parable who received rebuke did not *lose* any of his Master's money, he simply gave back the exact amount he received. God does not want us to return the same amount He gave us. He demands and deserves to receive what He gave us plus the interest we earn through hard work. Everything you need to know about how God sees the sloth is found in the conversation between the slothful servant and the Lord. Which servant do you want to be, the faithful or the slothful? Then get to work!

OVERCOMING THE INNER SLOTH

Nothing on earth lasts forever. This is a fact that governs all activities on this planet. I love to remind the teenagers in our youth group about this truth every year before we head to camp. Camp is a nine- to ten-hour bus ride that leaves the church at five in the morning. The ride is unpleasant, long, and uncomfortable. Every year when the complaining begins, I always remind the teenagers that no matter how bad the ride might be, it does not last forever.

There is a time restraint on your life. All activities of life are governed by time. At some point there is the beginning, and at some point there will be an end. Life is no different. Your life on earth had a beginning, and your life on earth will have an end. No surprise there. I doubt anyone is honestly hoping they have figured out immortality; yet, the truth is very few of us ever consider that the end of our lives may be near. You cannot honestly say that you will be alive tomorrow. In fact, you cannot guarantee that you will not die in a car accident or in a burglary gone wrong before you go to bed tonight. You could go to the doctor who diagnoses you with cancer or some other terrible sickness. Just think about it. How many people who die today knew that their lives would end today? The answer is none of them. I just recently saw on the news the story of two subway busses colliding outside a large U.S.

Metropolis during rush hour. The death count continues to rise as they sift through the wreckage. There were people on that train who were likely planning their evening activities or work projects who in moments lost their lives. Feel free to ask their families about the certainty of tomorrow.

Solomon points out this same motivating factor for us to get busy using our lives, talents, and time for the Lord. In Proverbs 27:1 Solomon writes, "Boast not thyself of to morrow; for thou knowest not what a day may bring forth." Do you know what I love about this life-changing truth? I love its simplicity. Plain and simple, don't count on being alive tomorrow, because you might not be. In this simple exhortation from the inspiration of God's Spirit procedes the motivation needed to overcome your inner sloth.

You might have begun this chapter living the life of a sloth. In fact, you might have read the first two sections and still refuse to do the work you know needs to be done. The reason for your stubbornness is that you want to enjoy living your way for a little longer. Once you have had your fun, then you will get things right and start preparing for your time of judgment. What if you died tonight? What if your plans for a future turnaround never happened? What if your life ended and you entered eternity next week? What would you have to show for your life?

If you had to stop and dig up something you could show for your life in order to answer that last question, then you are not ready to stand before God. That fact ought to make you shiver. God's Word is simple, honest, and just: you will stand before Him one day and give an account of your productivity in this life. If you live well, you will receive a commendation. If you squander your time on this earth in vain pursuits, you will receive the rebuke of a person who wasted the great blessings and talents of God. The Scriptures also teach that this time of accounting can come anytime. You are not guaranteed tomorrow or even tonight. Don't present God with a vineyard uncared for, overgrown, and with a broken-down wall. Don't waste your opportunity to present your King with glory and honor. Make a commitment with your King that from now on you will live to the best of your ability, working the work of God by using your gifts and cultivating your relationship with

God. Live in a way that breeds the confidence that if you were to face your time of accounting well before you expect to, you will present a beautiful vineyard that produced pleasing fruit for the Lord. It is the obvious choice; however, it is your choice. Which will you choose, the way of the sloth or the way of the diligent?

CHARTING YOUR COURSE

Lifeless Living is Barren Living

1. What term does Solomon use to describe a person living a lifeless life?

2. Is a sloth something you want to be compared to?

3. What are the three characteristics of slothful living?

   _____

   _____

   _____

4. Honestly, are any of these characteristics present in your life?

Key Passage to Memorize

Proverbs 21:25–26

God's View of the Sloth

1. Whose view should you be concerned about: the world's or God's?

2. The slothful in work is brother to whom? (Proverbs 18:9)

3. Which servant relates to the sloth in the parable in Matthew 25:14–30?

4. Do you want God to rebuke you the same way He rebuked that servant?

Key Passage to Memorize

Proverbs 18:9

Overcoming the Inner Sloth

1. Which of the three steps to living a successful Christian life (productivity, understanding your responsibilities, and being aware of the brevity of life) do you struggle with?

2. Would you honestly say your life is being productive for God?

3. Though it is not wrong to enjoy recreational and entertaining activities, are there some activities that take up too much of your time?

4. If so, then list the activities.

5. Are you guaranteed to be alive tomorrow?

6. How should this guarantee change the way you live?

7. If you were to face the Christian's judgment today, would you be excited or ashamed?

8. Read the following Scriptures and record your thoughts:

    a. Psalm 90:12

    b. 1 Corinthians 3:11–15

    c. 2 Corinthians 5: 9–10

    d. Ephesians 5:15–16

    e. James 4:14

9. Make a chart that will help you plan your activities each week. Make sure that along with school and your recreational activities you schedule a time with the Lord *every day* to read His word and pray. Also look for time *every week* when you plan can help with something specific in your church or youth group.

Key Passage to Memorize

Proverbs 27:1

OBSTACLE 5:
CARNAL COMMUNICATIONS

WISDOM'S CRY CONCERNING CHRISTIAN COMMUNICATION

It seems that every year or so a large wildfire tears through some part of the country. I remember a few years back when a wildfire was particularly bad. The news covered the fire and the progress of the firefighters on a daily basis. I can remember watching in shock and amazement the pictures of the thousands and *hundreds* of thousands of acres completely ravished by the flames. Further, I watched as people witnessed the destruction of their dream homes and possessions from a safe distance. I do not know if the reporter had researched the statement he was about to make, but I remember one reporter saying that this wildfire was the worst on record. As the weeks passed and the fire was extinguished, an investigation was launched into the beginning of the fire. The fire investigators were able to track the start of this devastating tragedy to a single camping spot. In the middle of this camping spot was a small dugout hole for a campfire. What the investigators believed happened was that a group of campers did not completely extinguish the campfire and a few of the embers were carried by the wind from the campfire to the woods, igniting one of the greatest wildfires on record.

As I listened to the official report, I found it incredible that such a large and devastating fire could be birthed from the remains of a small campfire. As I sat and listened, my mind ventured to the book of James. In his epistle, James speaks on the power and potency of the tongue. In chapter 3, verses 5 and 6, James writes, "Even so the tongue is a little member, and boasteth great things. Behold, how great a matter a little fire kindleth! And the tongue is a fire, a world of iniquity: so is the tongue among our members, that it defileth the whole body, and setteth on fire the course of nature; and it is set on fire of hell." James uses the picture of a small fire causing a great fire to show the great power and importance of our communications. However, James was not the first writer inspired by the Holy Spirit to record such truths.

Solomon wrote on the power of words, the problem with words, and the way to tame words in the book of Proverbs. The reason that God inspired passages on the importance of communication is because the power and potency of words do not change from generation to generation. What changes is human acceptance of the wrong usage of words. You live in a world in which freedom of speech is used to excuse sinful, anti-God, anti-Scripture language. This abuse of our "right" to speak our minds, no matter who we may hurt or how wrong we are, is commonly practiced among young people, even Christian young people.

I am sure you know exactly what I am talking about. You face situations on almost a daily basis in which you or someone you know is hurt because of someone else's words—either friends at school or in your church youth group. In dealing with these issues, I always hear someone say, "Well, she (or he) said _____." When I ask how he or she responded to the comment, I usually hear, "Then I said _____." The problem is that usually both of the blank spaces are filled with mean, cruel, and biting remarks formed with the intent to embarrass, hurt, and humiliate the recipient. There are some instances in which the teenagers involved refuse to forgive and move on, but most cases usually get settled. But even when the situations get settled, which involves apologies, forgiveness, tears, and hugs, the great power of the tongue is manifested. I know from experience, as do you, that the sting and memory of what was said will linger for years. I am sure you are all familiar with the terribly inaccurate statement, "Sticks and stones may break my bones, but words will never hurt me." The truth of the matter is that bones *will* heal; the wounds caused by words *may never* fully heal.

Knowing the power of the tongue and its danger to our society, it ought to be obvious that the next obstacle you must overcome to live a life that is pleasing to God is the obstacle of carnal communications. This obstacle comes with a great disclaimer: This is an obstacle that you will never fully overcome. Notice that James 3:8 says, "But the tongue can no man tame." I don't want you to get discouraged about this truth, but rather to see it as a challenge. Know that this obstacle will never go away. No matter where you go or how long you live, the obstacle of carnal communications will always remain. What this means for us is that we must make sure we learn about this obstacle from the Scriptures and prepare ourselves to be victorious.

THE POWER OF WORDS

A few years back, our youth group went on a mission trip to Washington D.C. It was wonderful! We had a great time with the teens and saw many people come to Christ. One of the more memorable moments came not in the events or in touring the monuments, but on the end of a ballpoint pen. During the tourism part of the trip we shopped at a lot of the little souvenir shops up and down the streets. One of the boys purchased a trick pen from a vender; it sent an electric shock into the hand of the person who tried to click the pen. I first noticed this pen when I saw the group of boys standing in a circle shocking one another to see who was the toughest. When invited to test *my* manhood, I chose to give it a try. Looking at the pen, it did not look dangerous; however, when I clicked the pen, the shock shot through my entire body! I tried to look as if it did not affect me, but I tell you, I will never underestimate one of those pens ever again.

Words can often appear as harmless and nonthreatening as the trick pen. I have heard people say that words are only words. This mentality camouflages the true power of words and opens us up to the danger of causing more harm and hurt feelings than we could ever imagine. God knows the power of words, and in order to help us understand the true power of words, God moved Solomon to record for us the great power of words both for good and for evil.

In Proverbs 18:21 Solomon writes, "Death and life *are* in the power of the tongue: and they that love it shall eat the fruit thereof." God records that your tongue has both the power of death and life. A lot of things have the power to kill. Some things used in the proper way have the ability to heal or retain life. But your tongue and the words of your mouth have the power to do both. On the end of this statement comes an admonition and a warning. God admonishes us that if we love the power of the tongue (i.e. use our tongue in a godly fashion), then we will eat the fruit it produces. To love the power of the tongue in this capacity will bring joy, happiness, and blessings according to the blessings of God. However, the warning is as true as the admonition. If you choose to hate the power of the tongue (i.e. use the power of the tongue in a sinful fashion), then understand you will also eat the fruit it produces. The fruit of sinful words will not bring pleasant blessings, but rather punishment and a season of painful reaping of what you have sown.

This admonition and warning is demonstrated throughout the teachings of Proverbs. I have listed these teachings of Proverbs concerning the power of the tongue to do good and to do evil to help you understand just how powerful your tongue is. Notice that in both cases, the power of the tongue is demonstrated in the consequences the different use of the tongue produces.

Power of the Tongue to Do Good
- The tongue of the wise is as choice silver. (Proverbs 10:20)

- The tongue of the wise feeds many. (Proverbs 10:21)

- A good word makes a heavy heart happy. (Proverbs 12:25)

- A soft answer can stop wrath. (Proverbs 15:1)

- Using your words in a godly way brings great joy. This tongue is very good! (Proverbs 15:23)

- "Pleasant words are as an honeycomb, sweet to the soul, and health to the bones." (Proverbs 16:24)

Power of the Tongue to Do Evil

- In the list of the seven abominations in the sight of God, Solomon mentions lying lips and the person who causes discord among Christians. (Proverbs 6:17, 19)

- The wicked is trapped by the sin of his lips. (Proverbs 12:13)

- Lying lips are an abomination to the Lord. (Proverbs 12:22)

- The person who does not control his tongue brings destruction on himself. (Proverbs 13:3)

- Words have the power to separate best friends. (Proverbs 16:28)

- The person with a perverse tongue falls into mischief. (Proverbs 17:20)

- Gossip will cause deep, lasting wounds. (Proverbs 18:8)

- A false witness will not go unpunished, and liars will not escape. (Proverbs. 19:5, 9)

- As wood gives life to fire, so gossip gives life to strife. (Proverbs 26:20)

- The lying tongue hates and afflicts people, and the flattering lips cause ruin. (Proverbs 26:28)

- Flattery leads into a trap. (Proverbs 29:5)

As I studied this list, I noticed something interesting. I noticed that the good use of the tongue benefits everyone, while the sinful use of your tongue destroys you. Let that sink into your heart. So often we choose to use sinful communication in order to get revenge on someone or hurt others. It is true that your words hurt others and will cause deep wounds; however, your sin will not only hurt you, it will *destroy* you. Look at the list. The Spirit of God warns that the wrong use of the tongue will lead you into traps, mischief, punishment, the anger of the Lord, hatred, strife, and ruin! Remember, this is God's truth not man's invention. This list of consequences has the approval seal of God. Heed the warning; do not underestimate the power of words. They can bring great joy and blessing to you and others or they can harm others and destroy you!

THE PROBLEM WITH WORDS

The power of the tongue reminds me of the power of electricity. Electricity can kill you, but used in the right way, it can also save your life. For instance, if you unfortunately walk on live power lines which were pulled down by a storm, electricity will kill you. However, if you have a heart attack and your heart stops beating, electricity can be used to restart your heart. In a sense, life and death are in the nature of electricity. The reason why electricity is considered dangerous is because the natural state of electricity brings death.

Electricity reminds me of the tongue because in the natural state of the tongue, it likewise causes death instead of life. Solomon records this problem with words in Proverbs 10:19. Solomon writes, "In the multitude of words there wanteth not sin." In modern terms, "The more you talk, the more you are likely to sin with your words." In Proverbs 13:3 Solomon wrote, "He that keepeth his mouth keepeth his life: but he that openeth wide his lips shall have destruction." Again, in modern terms, "If you want to live, you better think before you speak!" (I think I remember my mom saying something like that to me on more than one occasion.) In both of these passages, God's warning is clear: words naturally tend toward sin.

You might be wondering, "Why do words lean toward sin? Didn't God create communication? If God created it, why is it bad?" The answer is simple. You are sinful, and therefore everything that comes from you comes from your sinful nature. God did create man uniquely allowing us the gift of communication with each other and with Him. When God created Adam, communication was perfect. When Adam and Eve infused humanity with sin, communication took on the form of the communicator. God's communication is still perfect. God's Word is complete and without error in its original form. Human communication, however, is full of sin and therefore will lead to sin.

"Okay, I got this thing figured out! If the more I talk, the more chance I have of sinning, then I am just not going to talk." This remedy might sound appealing to those around you, but this is not the remedy God desires for your life. Remember, your tongue has the power to bless others and bring joy to your life. That is the original intention God has for communication. We cannot allow our sin nature and the sinful philosophy of the world to hinder our original responsibility toward God. God desires not silence, but success through the taming of your words.

THE TAMING OF WORDS

One aspect I love about my wife is her innate ability to jump from one subject to another completely unrelated subject in the midst of a conversation without warning. Several years ago I heard a man stop and make a comment about this tendency in *his* wife. He said, "Hold on, you were just talking about _____ and now you are talking about _____. Evel Knievel could not make that leap!" From that moment on, I began to joke with my wife when she follows suit (which by the way is a sign of fast thinking and therefore intelligence, lest any of you think I am demeaning women). I love to stop and say, "Wow, Evel Knievel could not make that leap; give me a second to catch up."

I mention this because you might be thinking, "We started this chapter with a challenge from James that no person can tame the tongue. Now you are telling us the way to overcome this obstacle and please the Lord with our lives is to tame the tongue. Pastor Nate, Evel Knievel could not make that leap. How are we supposed to reconcile the two?" You cannot tame your tongue, but God can! The taming of the tongue is a continual process that requires your growing dependence on God. The goal for us in this section is not a once-and-done process, but rather to provide biblical safeguards to help in the taming process. It is only through the setting up of these safeguards found in the power and Word of God that you will be able to tame your tongue.

SPEAK WHAT IS ACCEPTABLE

This safeguard is nothing more than common sense. You know what is right, and you know what is wrong. You know what is acceptable to say, and you know what is not acceptable to say. If you desire to be wise in the use of your tongue, you must know and speak that which is acceptable. In Proverbs 10:32 Solomon writes, "The lips of the righteous know what is acceptable: but the mouth of the wicked speaketh forwardness." This verse teaches about the two types of people you can be, depending on the way you use your tongue. If you desire to be righteous, then you will know what is acceptable and speak that. If you desire to be wicked, then you can use your tongue to talk about whatever you want. Which do you want to be? If you said righteous, then speak in a way that you already know is pleasing to God and do not allow the wicked perversions of this world to find a friend in your tongue.

Before we move on, allow me to give some extra help. Though the process to know and speak what is acceptable is simple in theory, the practice of it is anything but easy. This is why God warns us that our tongues are vile and wicked and impossible to completely control. There are several ways in which you can practically help yourself in the taming of your tongue. The most significant source of victory and defeat revolves around your friends. I know we have already looked at friendship, but bear with me. No one can influence you like your friends. If you surround yourself with people who constantly allow the filth of this world to flow from their mouth, you will follow suit. I have seen it time and time again. If you don't believe me, listen to the admonition of Solomon in Proverbs 20:19, "He that goeth about as a talebearer revealeth secrets: therefore meddle not with him that flattereth with his lips." Did you catch that? Solomon said through the inspiration of the Holy Spirit, "Don't meddle, don't mess with, don't be around those who use their tongue in an ungodly fashion!" Why would Solomon write this admonition? Simply put, the more you are around this type of person the more damage they will do to you and you will do to yourself. Do more than just *know* what is acceptable, *speak* that which is acceptable, and surround yourself with like-minded people.

THINK BEFORE YOU SPEAK

I can remember hearing this advice as a child from my parents, whom I am sure heard this phrase when *they* were children. The reason for the constant repetition of this phrase is the fact that this wise advice is contrary to our nature. When someone insults us or says something against what we think or believe, our immediate reaction is to lash back at them using our tongue as a weapon. How many times have we gotten ourselves in trouble because we refused to stop and think about what we are about to say?

As a father of children who are fifteen months apart, I see this principle in action every single day. I cannot tell you how often I have had to discipline one of the children because they chose to lash out with their mouth rather than allowing me or my wife to take care of it. When this happens, I always take the time to tell them that if they had allowed Mommy or Daddy to take care of the problem, they would not be disciplined. However, because they did not stop and think about what they were about to say, they put themselves in this position.

I am sure that Solomon was thinking upon different times in which he witnessed people lashing out without taking time to think when he penned, "A fool uttereth all his mind: but a wise man keepeth it in till afterwards" (Proverbs 29:11). Don't miss the fact that Solomon calls those who speak without thinking fools! As you read the book of Proverbs, you will understand that "fool" is not the way in which you want Solomon to describe you. Once again, notice the contrast, "But a wise man quietly holds it back."

Notice with me a second passage in which Solomon reaffirms this truth of Scripture. In Proverbs 17:27–28 Solomon writes, "He that hath knowledge spareth his words: and a man of understanding is of an excellent spirit. Even a fool, when he holdeth his peace, is counted wise: and he that shutteth his lips is esteemed a man of understanding." I hope that you can see the thread of truth connecting this whole study. Solomon wrote that in the multitude of words sin is easy to come by. He also wrote that those who speak without thinking are as good as fools, but a wise person will control his mouth. In this passage, Solomon again states that a person of knowledge and wisdom will spare his words. Even a fool (and you know how Solomon feels about fools) is considered a man of wisdom if he or she will shut his or her mouth and not speak rashly.

Before we bring this section to a close, I would like you to meditate on a harsh warning from the Spirit of God. "Seest thou a man that is hasty in his words? there is more hope of a fool than of him" (Proverbs 29:20). Stop and read that again. Here is your warning: If you do not strive to tame your tongue through common sense and discipline, there is more hope for a fool than for you!

The fifth obstacle you must overcome to live a life that is pleasing to God is the obstacle of carnal communications. This means that you must heed the Scripture's warnings to understand and appreciate the great power of words. Your tongue has the power to bring joy and blessings or pain and death. You must also realize the truth that as a sinful human being, your tongue's natural direction is the path of pain and death. If you desire to please God and fulfill His original intention for your tongue, you must strive to tame your tongue through knowing and speaking what is acceptable and right, always taking the time to think about what you are going to say. If you take this wisdom and apply it to your life, you will not be perfect, but you will save yourself untold misery and grief. Take up the challenge to be the best Christian communicator you can be for the glory of God!

CHARTING YOUR COURSE

The Power of Words
1. What two things are in the power of your tongue?
2. Have you ever experienced the joy of using your tongue for life? If yes, explain.

3. Have you ever experienced the pain of using your tongue for death? If yes, explain.

4. Are words harmless?

5. When you use your tongue for life, who benefits?

6. When you use your tongue for death, who gets destroyed?

Key Passage to Memorize

Proverbs 18:21

The Problem with Words

1. Do your words lean toward God or sin? Why?

2. Is not talking at all a good remedy for this problem? Why?

Key Passage to Memorize

Proverbs 10:19

The Taming of Words

1. Can you tame your tongue?

2. Can God tame your tongue?

3. Knowing this truth, whose power should you rest in for victory?

4. What are some acceptable things to talk about?

5. What are some unacceptable things to talk about?

6. Do your friends talk more about what is acceptable or unacceptable?

7. A great way to keep from sinning with your mouth is to _____ before you _____.

8. What does Solomon say about the fool who thinks before he speaks in Proverbs 17:27–28?

Key Passage to Memorize

Proverbs 29:20

OBSTACLE 6:
GODLESS GOALS

WISDOM'S CRY CONCERNING GOD-HONORING GOALS

A famous poem by Robert Frost describes a traveler coming to a fork in the road. As the traveler looked at each path, he understood that since he would not be in this position ever again, his choice would make an impact on the rest of his life. The poet records his observations about each of the paths. One path was commonly traveled on and bore the marks of a well-worn trail, while the other bore the marks of a less-worn trail. After much inner debate, the author chose to take the path that was less traveled on. At the end of the poem, Frost concludes the path choice made all the difference.

We have come a long way, and I pray that up to this point you have been honest with yourself and with God and taken the difficult steps necessary to live a life that is pleasing to the Lord. This sixth obstacle is the last external obstacle we are going to cover in this book. This obstacle is the obstacle of godless goals. In this chapter we will look at the choice you must make with regard to which path you will travel on in your life. There are two choices: the path of greed and worldly pleasure, or the path of righteousness. Since you will never be the same age again and in the same position you are now, your choice will affect the rest of your life.

Seeing that your future goals for life are important, it is no wonder that God moved Solomon to record a large amount of Scripture concerning your choice. In its most basic form, the choice you have to make is between the path of greed (selfish desires) and the path of righteousness (godly desires).

THE PATH OF GREED

Have you ever been asked a question with an obvious answer? Well, you just have! Ha! Anyway, back to the question. These questions are usually asked in an attempt to prove a point. For instance, I remember a commercial on television that had a man with two socks mounted on a board walking around asking people which sock was whiter. His point was to demonstrate which detergent worked better. The choice was obvious and when presented in the form it was, the audience could easily see which was better. But that is not real life. I wonder how many of those people would still choose that detergent when confronted with the higher price. The right answer would still be true; however, choosing to follow what is obvious is not as easy a task.

Your choice is much the same. If you had to pick now between the path of greed and the path of righteousness without ever looking at what the Scriptures teach concerning the two, you would likely choose the obvious path of righteousness. However, the problem is that the path of righteousness comes with a higher price initially and is therefore not usually the first choice of young people—even Christian young people. In fact, there are an overwhelming majority of Christians who are not walking on the path of righteousness but rather on the path of greed.

The call of the path of greed is so strong and common that Solomon mentions it in the first chapter of the book of Proverbs. In Proverbs 1:10–19 Solomon writes, "My son, if sinners entice thee, consent thou not. If they say, Come with us . . . We shall find all precious substance, we shall fill our houses with spoil: Cast in thy lot among us; let us all have one purse: My son, walk not thou in the way with them; refrain thy foot from their path . . . they lay wait for their own blood; they lurk privily for their own lives. So are the ways of every one that is greedy of gain." It is amazing to me that one passage of Scripture written nearly three thousand years ago contains all the elements of the path of greed's call to Christians today.

- Peer pressure (Proverbs 1:10)

- A call to forget morals (Proverbs 1:11–12)

- Promise of wealth and riches (Proverbs 1:13)

- Promise of friendship and partnership (Proverbs 1:14)

- Promise of great risk (Proverbs 1:16–19)

These are the same elements Satan used back in Solomon's time and still uses today. The better you can familiarize yourself with these elements and flag them, the easier it will be for you to recognize the wrong path in life. Let's break these down and add some supporting wisdom from Proverbs to understand how to combat Satan's tactics.

- Peer pressure
  We have already discussed what Solomon taught concerning friends. In Proverbs 13:20 Solomon teaches that the person who walks with wise men will be wise but a companion of fools will be destroyed. If your friends are pressuring you to do something wrong, then they are not your *friends* but *fools*. Know that God promises the companion of such people will face destruction.

- A call to forget morals
  This is a result of the peer pressure to do something wrong. Both you and the fools pressuring you know that what you are going to do is wrong and contrary to what God teaches. Solomon writes in Proverbs 14:2 that for you to continue on this perverse way knowing it is contrary to God's law is to "despise" the Lord. Let that sink into your heart. You know that the path that despises God is not a path you want to be on. It doesn't end well!

- Promise of wealth and riches
  This is perhaps the most alluring element in our day. America is obsessed with wealth, riches, and fame. It always breaks my heart when I ask someone what they want to do with their life, and they tell me they want to make a lot of money. That is not a godly goal!

Listen to what God has to say about wealth and riches. "Labour not to be rich: cease from thine own wisdom. Wilt thou set thine eyes upon that which is not? for riches certainly make themselves wings; they fly away as an eagle toward heaven (Proverbs 23:4–5). Their promise costs you lasting consequences for temporary wealth at best. Not a good deal in the eyes of God!

- Promise of friendship and partnership
  Again God says that to be companions of these men and women will bring destruction into your life. Is this promise really something you want? Your choice!

- Promise of great risk
  This last element is not one we like to hear out loud, however, according to Proverbs 1:16–19 with their call (the call of sinners according to verse 10) comes the great risk. Solomon writes that they wait for their own blood and will end up consuming their own lives. Do not miss this! If you choose to follow the path of greed, you will find yourself making risks that can ruin your life. Here is the problem: God tells us you reap what you sow. You will loose the risk and reap the horrible consequences.

At first glance, the path of greed looks attractive. It is wide, well-traveled, and well-accepted in our time. However, when we look at the call of the path of greed in light of the Scriptures, we see the true nature of this path. Satan's tactic is to focus on the path of greed and all the wonderful possibilities and pleasures it could yield. What Satan does not want you to know is that God *promises* in His Word that the path of greed will not only yield great unhappiness, but also that it will certainly lead to destruction and sorrow. Before I get ahead of myself, let's explore the end of the path of greed.

THE END OF GREED

The path of greed is appealing. Let's just be honest; people who make that choice will experience times of joy and what they consider success. I do not want you to think that anyone who chooses that path will be miserable their entire life. But what I am saying is that no matter what temporary joy they might experience, the consequences of their actions and lives will far outweigh any pleasure their sinful ways will produce.

Though Solomon speaks often on the devastation and destruction from the path of greed, there is a definite reoccurrence of God's warning concerning the direct consequences of personal sin. There are five different passages in which God's Spirit moves Solomon to record that a person's sin will be his or her prison of consequence. Notice them with me.

- "Therefore shall they eat of the fruit of their own way, and be filled with their own devices. For the turning away of the simple shall slay them, and the prosperity of fools shall destroy them." (Proverbs 1:31–32)

- "His own iniquities shall take the wicked himself, and he shall be holden with the cords of his sins." (Proverbs 5:22)

- "The integrity of the upright shall guide them: but the perverseness of transgressors shall destroy them." (Proverbs 11:3)

- "The backslider in heart will be filled with his own ways." (Proverbs 14:14*a*)

- "The robbery of the wicked shall destroy them." (Proverbs 21:7*a*)

Our God is a fair and just God. God allows us to choose which path we will walk on—the path of righteousness or the path of greed. And before we make our choice, God gives us a powerful warning: whichever you choose, you *will* have. It reminds me of when we took our children to a store and allowed them to choose a toy from the clearance section. One chose a cup and goggles and the other chose a toy microphone. Each child saw the options and made their choice based upon what they thought they wanted. It was not long however until they were both fighting over the microphone. You see, the one who chose the cup and goggles thought she was getting a better deal, but when she realized the fun her brother was having with the microphone, she suddenly wanted it instead. The problem was that she picked out her toys, and the microphone was not one of the toys she picked. She did not *get* the microphone, because she did not *choose* the microphone; she kept her cup and goggles because they were the toys she chose.

In the same way you will have the consequences of whichever path you choose. If you want to choose the path of greed, then understand that the people you surround yourself with will be the people who will hurt you. The sins you allow in your life will be the chains that bind you in the end. You *will have* exactly what you choose. If that thought does not make you stop and consider your path, perhaps the next thought will.

Often when we think of the end of our path on this earth, we think of our death. It is true that your path on the earth ends when you die, however, the consequences of your choices live on after you are gone. If you choose the path of greed, understand that your family will be affected for generations to come. The Spirit of God translates this truth when He inspired, "The memory of the just is blessed, but the name of the wicked shall rot" (Proverbs 10:7). You will leave a legacy with your life. Whether that legacy leaves a memory that is blessed or a memory that brings anger and sorrow is a choice you will make when you choose which path to travel. Know this, if the people who have chosen the path of greed could see what they would reap for their actions, they would never have taken that first step in the wrong direction.

Take the story of Cain in Genesis 4. Cain and his brother Abel both presented their offerings to the Lord. God accepted Abel's but did not accept Cain's because it was not what God commanded. Cain became angry and even though God warned him about the desire of sin and the consequences of the wrong choice, Cain chose to travel the path of his own desires, and he killed his brother, Abel. Take note and let the personal torment of the words of Cain fill you heart and mind with the fear of the Lord. In verse 13, after hearing what his actions reaped in his life, Cain cried, "My punishment is greater than I can bear." If Cain had known the consequences for the path he traveled before traveling it, he would never have taken that first step.

My friends, you have God's warning in the Scriptures as well as the examples of men and women who have reaped the awful end of the path of greed. If you could know the terrible consequences your actions will bring, you would stop and think about taking the wrong path. The call of the path of greed may be exciting and full of promise; the end leaves you bound and destroyed by your own choices and causes your legacy to live as a memorial of your wickedness for as long as your children live.

THE PATH OF RIGHTEOUSNESS

After examining the path of greed, the obvious choice for any Christian is most definitely not the path of greed. However, before we can choose the path of righteousness, we must be able to recognize it. If we do not know what the path of righteousness consists of, then how can we know if we are indeed living on the path of righteousness?

WHAT DOES THE PATH OF RIGHTEOUSNESS LOOK LIKE?

The first and perhaps most important element of the path of righteousness is the element of complete trust in God. Solomon teaches this principle in one of Proverbs' most well-known passages. In Proverbs 3:5–6 Solomon writes, "Trust in the Lord with all thine heart; and lean not unto thine own understanding. In all thy ways acknowledge him, and he shall direct thy paths."

Complete trust is the first element of walking on the path of righteousness. Though we could sit and talk a long time concerning the different elements of trusting with all your heart, trusting more than your own understanding, and trusting in every situation, it all comes down to this: do you trust God? Do you trust God in every area of your life? I did not ask if you trust God in *some* areas but *all* areas of life. Do you trust God to lead you where He wants you to go, no matter how you may feel about it? Do you trust God when bad things happen to those you love? Do you trust God to protect and reward you when you follow what the Scriptures teach? If you could not answer "yes" to all of these questions, then you are not walking on the path of righteousness. It is only as you allow your heart to trust God without reservation that you can understand and claim the following promise: "and he shall direct thy paths." Think of it this way, you cannot follow the road signs to get to your goal, if you are not traveling on the road.

The second element of the path of righteousness is an element geared to keep you walking on the path of righteousness. This second element is walking in prudence or caution. If you want to follow the road signs that lead to righteousness, then you need to stay on the road. To stay on the road, you need to travel in a way that will keep you on the road. Starting out on the road of righteousness is great; however, if you do not finish on the road to righteousness, your beginning will not matter. Staying on the road is a task easier said than accomplished.

Though this is not an easy task, this task does not require much more than applying common sense to your life. In order to guide you along the path of righteousness, the Spirit of God moved Solomon to record a similar warning in three passages in Proverbs.

- "A wise man feareth, and departeth from evil: but the fool rageth, and is confident." (Proverbs 14:16)

- "A prudent man foreseeth the evil, and hideth himself: but the simple pass on, and are punished." (Proverbs 22:3)

- "A prudent man foreseeth the evil, and hideth himself; but the simple pass on, and are punished." Proverbs 27:12

These three passages, two of which are identical, all teach the same truth. If you desire to remain on the path of righteousness, you need to be able to open your eyes, recognize the evil, and potential evil, in people and situations, and steer clear of the evil. This goal sounds simple enough, but there are times when this road is icy.

Growing up in Oklahoma, I did not have a lot of experience driving on icy roads. This fact was evident my senior year of high school. That year we had a massive ice storm that left six inches of ice all over the place. During the daytime the roads were manageable, and so in the afternoon I went to see a friend who lived way out in the country. I did not choose to come home until after the sun had set and a second blast of winter weather began. Not wanting to stay overnight, I chose to drive home. I never made it. It was an experience that I will never forget. I felt as if I was disoriented, because I could see the road and the ice, but I could not keep my vehicle from swerving and finally running into the ditch. My goal was simple, stay on the road and arrive at home, but achieving my goal required much more dedication than I could have imagined.

Achieving this second element of the path of righteousness is equally simple yet difficult. It is not difficult for you to see and recognize evil and spiritually dangerous situations and people. You have the intelligence to be able to see something that is not right and that has the potential to knock you off the path. Taking that wisdom and applying it to your everyday life is another thing altogether. If you want to stay on the path of righteousness and reap all the rewards God promises, then you need to be honest with yourself! You need to get serious about what you allow and what you do not allow into your eyes, ears, and relationships. It is only when you take the Word of God and use it as a filter that you will be able to remain on the path of righteousness. Only you, through the power of God's Word and Spirit, can grab hold of the steering wheel of your life and guide your vehicle down the road to arrive at home. Know that through God you can do this, but don't allow yourself to be fooled. It will be difficult!

The first element is complete trust in the Lord, the second element is walking in prudence (with caution), and the third element of the path of righteousness is generosity. Generosity is an element completely contrary to the thinking and philosophy of this world. Generosity also seems to be the odd duck in this discussion of the path of righteousness. You might be thinking, "Why do you think generosity should be considered part of the path of righteousness? Giving is not a spiritual thing. Anyone can give. What makes it so important for me to be generous?" That is a fair question, and to be honest with you, I did not originally intend to cite generosity as an element on the path of righteousness. It was not until I was studying the book of Proverbs in depth that the Spirit of God kept opening my heart to the many passages of Proverbs in which God inspired instruction concerning the generosity of a Christian. The more I studied, the more I realized that generosity is a great barometer to reveal which path you are walking. There are nine different passages in Proverbs in which Solomon deals directly with the subject of God's blessing on those who give to the poor. Solomon writes that he or she who gives: earns great riches

(Proverbs 13:7), gains happiness (Proverbs 14:21), is honored by God (Proverbs 14:31), will be repaid by God (Proverbs 19:17), will receive blessing (Proverbs 22:9), will receive the riches of those who are wicked (Proverbs 28:8), and will never lack (Proverbs 28:27). On the flip-side, God moved Solomon to record that a person who refused to be generous mocks God (Proverbs 17:5), and God will not hear his prayer (Proverbs 21:13).

It is clear that God speaks of the blessings of those who are generous and the consequences for those who refuse to be generous. Generosity yields blessings whereas greed (the opposite of generosity) brings reproach and awful consequences. Beginning with that thought, it is not difficult to understand that if a person refuses to be generous, then that person is not right with God. And if a person is not right with God, then that person is not walking on the path of righteousness.

The path of righteousness is made up of complete trust in the Lord, an attitude of prudence or caution in our walk, and a generous spirit. Though one can argue there are many more elements in the path of righteousness, one thing is for sure, if you are lacking any of the three elements listed in this section, you are not walking on the right path. We have already seen what the wrong path brings into our lives, so I will not repeat that. What I want to do instead is show you what God promises for those who remain on the path of righteousness to the end.

THE END OF RIGHTEOUSNESS

In the beginning, the path of righteousness does not seem as appealing as the path of greed. Who in their right mind would willingly choose to take the path of more discipline, less popularity, and seemingly less success if they both ended the same? God ensures us that the path of greed and the path of righteousness do not end the same. As we already saw, the path of greed ends with a person feasting on a plate of God's wrath and consequences as a result of selfish, sinful choices that marked every stage of his life. All riches are gone, and he leaves nothing but a sour and marred legacy.

God promises that the end of the path of righteousness is greater than any earthly "treasure." The rewards of a life lived on the path of righteousness are rewards that no amount of money or earthly pleasure can produce.

Something I find interesting is that Solomon wrote about these rewards for the path of righteousness thousands of years ago. Even with all of the changes over all those years, these incentives or goals are still treasured and highly pursued by our world today. Though the world follows many different avenues in hopes of achieving these rewards, they do so without success. Solomon teaches us exactly how we can receive these rewards.

The first reward that the path of righteousness produces is a guarantee of reward. Solomon writes in Proverbs 11:18, "The wicked worketh a deceitful work: but to him that soweth righteousness shall be a sure reward." Solomon uses the analogy of sowing and reaping to demonstrate the end of the Christian's choices. As we have seen, the path of greed produces a harvest of sorrow and pain, but in this passage Solomon teaches that the person who sows righteousness reaps a guaranteed reward. If you discipline yourself and choose to honor God with your goals, you will reap a wonderful reward. That reward consists of rewards we are going to look at as well as additional rewards found elsewhere throughout the Scriptures. The main emphasis of this first reward is the fact or the surety that you will receive your reward. God *will* reward those who honor Him with their lives. That is a fact that will never change.

The guarantee of this reward contrasts with a letter I recently received in the mail. When I opened this letter, I found a statement of congratulations for winning a wonderful prize. The more I read this letter, the more it appeared to be legitimate, and so I called the phone number listed on the letter for more information. What I discovered was though the letter guaranteed a prize or reward, that reward was not truly guaranteed. To receive the reward I was required to do several things, and then upon completion of these set tasks, my name would then be entered into the final prize drawing. If my name was not drawn, I went home empty-handed. That was not a guaranteed reward; that was a scam.

The reward God promises is a guarantee. If you sow righteousness with your life, you will receive a guaranteed reward. There are no extra activities or final drawings. Your reward is yours! Just as your consequences of sorrow and pain are guaranteed if you choose the path of greed, your sure reward from heaven is guaranteed if you choose the path of righteousness.

The second reward the path of righteousness yields is the reward of worry-free living. Note that I did not say *care*-less living, but worry-free living. The difference is in attitude. To live in a careless way is to not have proper regard for your responsibilities in life as a citizen, family member, and Christian. To live a worry-free life is to live fulfilling your responsibilities completely trusting in the promise of God that He will provide for you and protect you in all your ways. The incredible aspect about worry-free living is the fact that it is based not in ignorance but in knowledge. You as a Christian can live your life worry-free in the midst of this anxious world by claiming the truth of the words of Solomon.

In Proverbs 10: 2–3 Solomon writes, "Treasures of wickedness profit nothing: but righteousness delivereth from death. The Lord will not suffer the soul of the righteous to famish: but he casteth away the substance of the wicked." The Spirit of God records that all the treasures a wicked person can gain through wickedness profit nothing, but the end of righteousness is a freedom from death. Further, God promises that He will not allow the soul of a righteous man to hunger or want for food and needs, but all the provision of the wicked will be cast away.

Stop and think about those two promises. If you walk on the path of righteousness, you do not have to worry about provision or death. God promises you that He will provide for all your needs, and He comforts you with the knowledge that He will save you from death. With those two promises, what is there to worry about? What wonderful rewards the path of righteousness yields!

The final reward for those who choose the path of righteousness is a godly legacy. Your life will leave a legacy. Let's return to a verse we visited when we discussed the legacy of those who choose the path of greed. In Proverbs 10:7, Solomon writes, "The memory of the just is blessed, but the name of the wicked shall rot." We looked at the negative promise of this verse; now let's look at the positive. The Holy Spirit promises that the memory of the just is blessed. Further, in Proverbs 20:7 Solomon writes that the children of the just man are blessed after him. I hope you grasp the true greatness of this reward. You are mortal. One day all your work on this planet will be finished; and on that day all your wealth will be dispersed, all your possessions divided, and, at best, your accomplishments in the secular realm will be recorded on a plaque that will hang dormant on some wall and will eventually be placed in storage. However, if you choose to live your life on the path of righteousness, when you die, your legacy continues to bless and minister to your family and friends. If you become a parent, you will discover the God-given desire to give your children the best you can. Understand that this promise is the fulfillment of that desire. You can save up money for your children that will be spent. You can pay for your child's college, but that will fade. If you leave a godly legacy when you die, your children will never forget, and God promises that your legacy will bless them. What greater reward could God give us than the reward of a godly memory and legacy? Praise God for the end of the path of righteousness!

I would like to leave you with one final thought on God-honoring goals. This thought is found in Proverbs 30:7–9 and really summarizes the prayer of a Christian seeking God honoring goals. As you read this passage, I pray that you will take these words and make them real in your own hearts and minds. I call this passage my prayer of sufficiency. This prayer simply states the cry of wisdom concerning the paths of greed and righteousness. With this perspective, you can overcome this obstacle and live a life pleasing to the Lord.

Proverbs 30:7–9 "Two things have I required of thee; deny me them not before I die: Remove far from me vanity and lies: give me neither poverty nor riches; feed me with food convenient for me: Lest I be full, and deny thee, and say, Who is the LORD? or lest I be poor, and steal, and take the name of my God in vain."

CHARTING YOUR COURSE

The Path of Greed

1. Why does the path of greed seem so appealing at the start?

2. What does Solomon tell us in Proverbs 1:10–19 we should do if sinners entice us?

3. Who is responsible to make this choice?

4. What is the last element of the path of greed that you should always remember?

Key Passage to Memorize

Proverbs 1:10

The End of Greed

1. What provides the person's prison of consequences at the end of the path of greed? (There are five passages listed in the chapter concerning this truth.)

2. What impression does the memory of the person who chooses the path of greed leave to those after him?

Key Passage to Memorize

Proverbs 5:22

The Path of Righteousness

1. What is the first element of walking on the path of righteousness found in Proverbs 3:5–6?

2. Do you trust God? Would you trust Him if He allowed a lot of bad things to happen to you?

3. The second element on the path of righteousness is walking with _____ (caution).

4. Why is it important to be able to look for the danger ahead in your life?

5. What is the third element in walking on the path of righteousness?

6. What are the benefits of generosity?

7. What are the consequences of not being generous?

Key Passage to Memorize

Proverbs 3:5–6

The End of Righteousness

1. What is it about the reward for those who walk on this path that is so wonderful?

2. Does God ever break His guarantees?

3. Is worry-free living the same as careless living?

4. What is the difference?

5. What two things do those who walk on the path of righteousness not need to worry about?

6. What is the final reward for those who walk on the path of righteousness?

Key Passage to Memorize

Proverbs 10:2–3

OBSTACLE 7:
HARMFUL HUMANITY

WISDOM'S CRY CONCERNING PERSEVERANCE

In one of the greatest literary works of all time, Robert Louis Stevenson writes into his story a mystifying twist. This work introduces a character who is innately good. As the work continues, this character experiments on himself and creates an evil monster. These two characters battle each other throughout the entirety of the work. The captivating aspect about the battle between these two characters is the fact that the characters are the same man. The good desires and the bad desires wage war against each other in order to gain control of the man. The results of this battle lead to times of great joy as well as great sorrow, great victory as well as great defeat, and great purpose in life as well as directionless chaos in the main character's life.

This plot not only makes for great reading, but also makes for a great illustration of the battle raging inside every Christian. If you have read this work and taken the teaching of God's Word to heart, then your life resembles that of this main character. You have a desire and a determination to do what is right with your life and bring honor and glory to your Heavenly Father. The problem is that within all of us is a terrifying monster the Scriptures refer to as the flesh. The purpose of this monster is not honoring God but pleasing self. You likely have already discovered this monster inside of yourself and have fallen time and time again to its determination to please itself. If so, don't be discouraged; the greatest Christian man in the history of the church not only battled against this great monster, but recorded his real-life struggle in the Scriptures. The apostle Paul records his struggle with the flesh in Romans 7:14–25. There Paul tells us that there is another member in his body warring against his spirit for control of his actions (verse 23). This war causes him to do and say things that he knows are wrong, and it keeps him from doing and saying what he knows is right. In verse 18a the apostle recognizes and calls this monster by its name when he writes, "For I know that in me (that is, in my flesh,) dwelleth no good thing."

I love this passage because Paul, the great apostle, does not hold back the truth. He writes clearly about his struggle with his flesh. I recorded this passage for you because I want you to find encouragement in your own struggle. If Paul struggled, so will you. Do not lose hope because you struggle, but rather, prepare yourself for the day of battle so that you will gain the victory in life. You are human, therefore you have the monster of flesh living inside of you. There will be times in which your flesh defeats your spiritual will and brings you into defeat. That is a fact of life. You are not, and will never be, a perfect human. As such, you must seek the counsel of God concerning how you can prepare for victory over such a vicious enemy. For you to gain this victory in life, you must heed the cry of wisdom concerning perseverance.

RECOGNIZE DANGER AND AVOID IT

The first step on your journey toward perseverance is being able to recognize the danger ahead and avoid it. If you will take the time to cultivate and instill this first step into your life, you will win the victory over many of the obstacles you will face in life before the battle even begins. This step may sound familiar because it is closely linked to part of our discussion in the previous chapter. Notice what Solomon writes concerning the ability to recognize danger ahead of time and make the means to avoid it. In Proverbs 22:3 Solomon writes, "A prudent man foreseeth the evil, and hideth himself: but the simple pass on, and are punished." Does this sound familiar? It is the same verse we used in the previous chapter concerning walking prudently. This first step is the same principle as walking prudently. For you to succeed in perseverance, you must understand the truth that the more you fail, the more difficult it can be to continue. If you, however, as a prudent person, learn to recognize potential battles and failures in your path ahead, then you can avoid the battle and keep yourself from risking defeat.

This important step is a simple step to understand. It reminds me of a lesson I learned the hard way. Not long ago I was attempting to run a few errands. As I approached a familiar shortcut, I saw a sign that posted: "Road closed to thru traffic one mile ahead." I was familiar with this shortcut and knew there was some construction going on, but instead of heeding the warning, I chose to risk it and continued on my way. As I drew closer and closer to the shortcut, I saw at least two more signs posting that the road would be closed. I ignored those signs and continued on my way. Amazingly, I found that at the end of the mile, the road was indeed closed to through traffic. My shortcut quickly turned into a time-consuming voyage as I had to turn around and backtrack.

If I had simply paid attention to the warning signs, I would have been able to avoid the construction area closed to traffic. I chose to ignore both the warning signs and common sense; I risked that the signs were wrong, and I would be okay. It did not work for me that day, and it will never work for us in our spiritual journey in life. You have learned from your experience in life where danger awaits you. You know the people, the places, and the things that spell out danger for your spiritual life. You have experienced the failure from falling time and time again. Your past experiences mark your future course with warning signs of coming danger. What you must do as the prudent person is recognize the danger and alter your course before you find yourself staring at a spiritual "road closed" sign.

Wisdom's cry concerning perseverance begins with the practice of foresight that leads to change. If you desire to live a life that is pleasing to God and to overcome the obstacle of hopeless humanity, the first step you must take is making a commitment to read and heed the spiritual warning signs in your life. If you choose to do this, I promise you will find yourself in far fewer valleys of defeat. And the less time you spend in those valleys, the easier it will be for you to persevere.

LISTEN AND LEARN FROM YOUR MISTAKES

The second step in wisdom's cry concerning perseverance is learning from your mistakes. The reality is that we are all humans and there will be times in all of our lives in which the monster of flesh defeats our will to do good and plunges us into sin. When this happens, you will have a choice to make. You can either continue on in the valley of defeat, or heed the instruction of the Lord and press on toward victory. The options sound as if this choice would be a no-brainer; however, if you are not prepared to battle with Scripture the discouragement that spiritual failure brings, you will find it much easier and more appealing to continue in the valley of sin. The goal of life should be never to fall into the sin that comes from spiritual defeat.

Heeding the instruction of God is not as easy or simple as it may sound. In fact, more often than not, it is the instruction of God that makes the valley of sin seem appealing. The reason for this is that often the instruction of the Lord comes in the form of rebuke and reproof from others, some of whom genuinely care for us. The Holy Spirit tells us that if we are wise we will listen and learn from these people, but if we are foolish, we will despise their advice and find destruction. Note several passages authored by Solomon that share this truth.

- "Reprove not a scorner, lest he hate thee: rebuke a wise man, and he will love thee. Give instruction to a wise man, and he will be yet wiser: teach a just man, and he will increase in learning." (Proverbs 9:8–9)

- "A reproof entereth more into a wise man than an hundred stripes into a fool." Proverbs 17:10

- ". . . when the wise is instructed, he receiveth knowledge." Proverbs 21:11*b*

The admonition is clear: if you are wise, you will receive and apply the instruction and reproof of those who care for you. The problem is not the instruction of the Lord, but rather our flesh's response to the instruction. When the Lord allows others to help guide us in our way, our flesh unleashes its most dangerous attack—pride.

I have yet to find a living, breathing human being who likes being told he or she is wrong. I know that there have been times when I knew I was wrong but would not admit it because of pride. You know exactly what I am talking about. There are times when you know you are wrong but refuse to admit it. The strong feeling inside your heart and mind that refuses to admit wrong is called pride. Pride is a vicious monster that will destroy your will to listen to the instruction of the Lord, and it will chain you in the valley of sin. Of the many topics Solomon wrote, few are as widely mentioned as pride. Here is just a sample of references.

- God hates a proud look. (Proverbs 6:16–17)

- The fear of the Lord is to hate pride. (Proverbs 8:13)

- Pride brings shame. (Proverbs 11:2)

- Contentions only come as a result of pride. (Proverbs 13:10)

- Pride goes before destruction and a haughty spirit before a fall. (Proverbs 16:18)

- A person's pride will bring him low. (Proverbs 29:23)

God hates pride. Pride will lead you into destruction and will bring pain and sorrow into your life. Pride is the flesh's weapon that wars against the hearing and accepting of the instruction of God. If we do not battle against our pride and overcome its power in our lives, we will remain in the valley of sin and continue to make the same mistakes over and over because we refuse to learn from our mistakes.

You might be thinking, "That does not sound great, but it does not sound all *that* bad. I think I would rather try and find my own way out of that valley than listen to what this person who cares for me has to say!" If these thoughts rightly describe your own attitude, then allow me to reveal to you the future of the person who allows pride to keep him from hearing the reproof of the Lord. In Proverbs 15:10 Solomon writes, "Correction is grievous unto him that forsaketh the way: and he that hateth reproof shall die." In Proverbs 29:1 the Spirit of God inspires Solomon to write, "He, that being often reproved hardeneth his neck, shall suddenly be destroyed, and that without remedy."

The Scriptures teach that all that awaits a person who refuses to listen to the instruction of the Lord and learn from his own sin is death and sudden destruction. The foolishness of a person who would willingly choose such ends is beyond understanding. It would be like driving down the road and seeing a road sign that reads, "Certain death this way" with an arrow pointing to a cliff. In response you alter your course and drive off the cliff and die. No person in his right mind would make such a choice! Yet, the Scriptures teach clearly that if you decide to choose not to listen to the instruction of the Lord, you are changing the direction of your life and heading for the cliff of death and sudden destruction. If you desire to overcome the obstacle of hopeless humanity and live a life that is pleasing to God, then you must allow humility to replace pride in your heart and listen to the reproof and instruction of the Lord.

GET BACK ON YOUR FEET AND KEEP GOING

For you to overcome the obstacle of hopeless humanity and live a life that is pleasing to God you must recognize the dangers and attempt to avoid them, learn from your mistakes when you fail, and finally get back on your feet and keep going. This third step is the logical continuation in this process. What good will it do you if after you fail and learn from your mistake, you never attempt to keep living for God?

As a father, I make many mistakes with my children. When I make these mistakes, I apologize and mark them as areas for improvement. Then I do something interesting; I keep being a father. I do not quit. I do not throw in the towel after my mistakes, pack my bags, and walk out of the house never to return. I apologize, get right with God and my family, and I keep fulfilling my role as a father.

This truth of this third step is the same as the principle of being a father. When you fall into sin, take the time to listen to the instruction of the Lord whether through His Word, His Spirit, or one of His servants. Learn from your mistakes, and then get back on your feet and continue fulfilling your role as a Christian. This process is what separates you from the wicked in this world. Note what Solomon writes in Proverbs 24:16, "For a just man falleth seven times, and riseth up again: but the wicked shall fall into mischief." I love to share this verse with Christians who get discouraged by their sin. The Spirit of God says that a person who falls continually *and gets back up* is a "just man." God knows that you are going to sin. God knows that you are going to fall. God understands our sin and does not focus on our falling but rather on whether we get back up or remain in our sin. You might say, "That's great, but I fall more than seven times a day! How can God still forgive my sin and allow me to get back up?" I don't know how He can still forgive us, but I know that He does. That brings up a very important question: how can we get back on our feet as Christians and continue after learning from our mistakes?

When we fall, there is a process that we must abide by in order to get back on our feet. It is like when I broke my ankle one summer playing football. After I broke my ankle, I realized playing football in a gym wearing low-top tennis shoes was a bad idea. Even though I learned this lesson, it was not like I could just stand up and walk. I had to wait for my ankle to heal, and then I had to abide by the rules the doctor gave me for therapy and further healing. When we as Christians fall, we do not simply stand back up, but rather we must abide by the instructions God gives us to find forgiveness. Solomon records this God-ordained process in Proverbs 28:13, "He that covereth his sins shall not prosper: but whoso confesseth and forsaketh them shall have mercy."

God does not require us to work away the penalty of our sins, nor does He demand we do a lot of good works to outweigh our sin. God states for us plain and simple that if we desire to get back on our feet, we must first confess our sin and then forsake our sin.

Elsewhere in the Scriptures God promises that "if we confess our sins, he is faithful and just to forgive us our sins and to cleanse us from all unrighteousness" (1 John 1:9). When God forgives us, He promises to separate us from our sin and never again remember our sin (Psalm 103). When we confess our sin, God forgives our sin.

If confession leads to forgiveness, why then does the Spirit of God write that we must also forsake our sin? Think of it this way. Let's say that you get caught up in a foolish game of dare. The game ends suddenly when someone dares you to drink rat poison, and you are rushed to the emergency room. The doctors are able to pump your stomach and save your life. After the trip home, aside from a little soreness, your body is free from all effects of the poison. After you arrive home, you go back to your room and drink more poison, reasoning that the doctors already fixed the problem, and so it could not hurt to do it again. That would not be intelligent. If you were to do that, you would once again be rushed to the emergency room and have your stomach pumped. You would have to undergo this process every time you drank the poison. If you do not want to continue this painful process, then stop drinking the poison.

The same principle is true with your sin. When you sin, you should rush yourself to the spiritual emergency room of God's mercy seat and ask for forgiveness. When you receive forgiveness, you must not return to the same sin that brought you there in the first place but rather learn your lesson from your fall and put that sin as far away from you as possible. If you do not forsake your sin and place it far from you, you will soon find yourself back at the mercy seat pleading for the healing of God. Confession brings forgiveness and allows you to stand back up; forsaking keeps you on your feet living for God.

When you fall, it is imperative that you follow God's instructions and get back on your feet. Remember, the Spirit of God does not say that a just man is a perfect man, nor does Solomon write that a just man is a man that does not fall a lot. No, God's Word teaches that a just man is a man or woman who *when* he or she falls (no matter how many times), gets back up again. Don't forget the contrast between the just and the wicked. In that same passage the Scriptures record that a wicked person falls and remains. If you desire to be a just person in the eyes of God, then you must confess your sin, forsake your sin, and get back up to continue living for God.

Discouragement is part of the Christian life. Inside every human being is what the Scriptures call the flesh. Our flesh nature is in rebellion against God and the things of God. Our flesh is not like the other obstacles; this obstacle is part of us. We have a monster living inside of us waging war against our spirit to gain control of our actions and perform sinful acts contrary to the glory of God. We must look ahead and recognize the dangers of our path and try to avoid them at all costs. If we can avoid the battle, then we can prevent the risk of defeat. However, when we fail—and we *will* fail—we must humble ourselves and listen to the reproof and instruction of the Lord. After we learn our lesson, we must confess and forsake our sin, get back up on our feet, and continue on the path of righteousness. Remember, perseverance is not perfection; it is working to keep defeat and failure from stopping your progress for the Lord.

CHARTING YOUR COURSE

Recognize Danger and Avoid It

1. True or false: Recognizing the danger in the road ahead can help prevent battles from taking place.

2. The more you fail, the more _____ it can be for you to continue.

3. What warning signs has your past produced for your future walk?

4. What will happen if you ignore these signs?

5. Where else can you find spiritual warning signs to prevent you from falling into sin?

Key Passage to Memorize

Proverbs 22:3

Listen and Learn from Your Mistakes

1. Can you live a perfect life?

2. What is the difference between a wise person and a fool when it comes to listening to correction?

3. What is the main weapon of our flesh that wars against listening to correction?

4. How does God feel about pride?

5. Is your reaction to correction full of pride or humility? (Be honest.)

Key Passage to Memorize

Proverbs 15:10

Get Back on Your Feet and Keep Going

1. Does God want you to give up when you fail?

2. According to Proverbs 28:13, what is the two-step process needed to get back on our feet?

3. Why is it important not only to confess our sin but also to forsake our sin?

4. What is the difference between a just man who falls seven times and a wicked man who falls into mischief?

5. What does that tell you about the way God sees you? Does He care more about your falling or your getting back up?

Key Passage to Memorize

Proverbs 24:16

CONCLUSION

Life is full of spiritual obstacles that can wreck your voyage of pleasing God. If you desire to live a life that is pleasing to God and that is full of the benefits of wisdom, then you must seek the wisdom that is found in the fear of the Lord. The fear of the Lord is the beginning of wisdom, and wisdom is the key to overcoming the spiritual obstacles in life.

But wisdom is not the only benefit that comes with the fear of the Lord. Solomon writes in Proverbs 14:26–27, "In the fear of the Lord is strong confidence: and his children shall have a place of refuge. The fear of the Lord is a fountain of life, to depart from the snares of death." Another wonderful benefit produced by the fear of the Lord is confidence. When you humble yourself and seek the Lord, you will gain a confidence in life greater than anything this world can produce. Your confidence will come not in the wealth and security of this world but in the knowledge of the protection and provision of the Lord. As Solomon wrote, you will have a place of refuge. This refuge is in the hands and presence of the Almighty God. The more you understand the awe inspiring respect for your God, the more confidence you will gain to live a life pleasing in His sight.

The last benefit I want to leave you with is the fountain of life produced by the fear of the Lord. Solomon writes that this fountain will help you avoid the traps in life. This book calls these traps obstacles. Proverbs 14:26–27 restates the purpose of this book; however, it gives an illustration helpful for your understanding. Solomon calls this source of overcoming a fountain of life.

You are familiar with the saying, "You can lead a horse to water, but you cannot make him drink." *What's Stopping You?* has done nothing more than reveal the wonderful truths of the wisdom found in the book of Proverbs. This wisdom is the fountain of life that will help you avoid the traps and obstacles of life. You now have the knowledge of this fountain. The question is, will you drink from the wisdom of God and overcome the obstacles? Will you apply the wisdom of God and live a life pleasing to Him?

It is your choice. Drink deep, my friend!